NorthStar 2
LISTENING AND SPEAKING
THIRD EDITION

AUTHORS

Laurie Frazier

Robin Mills

SERIES EDITORS

Frances Boyd

Carol Numrich

PEARSON
Longman

NorthStar: Listening and Speaking Level 2, Third Edition

Pearson Education, 10 Bank Street, White Plains, NY 10606

Contributor credit: Linda Lane, American Language Program at Columbia University, authored and edited PRONUNCIATION material for *NorthStar: Listening and Speaking Levels 1–5, Third Edition.*

Staff credits: The people who made up the *NorthStar: Listening and Speaking Level 2, Third Edition* team, representing editorial, production, design, and manufacturing, are Aerin Csigay, Dave Dickey, Ann France, Gosia Jaros-White, Maya Lazarus, Melissa Leyva, Sherry Preiss, Robert Ruvo, Debbie Sistino, and Paula Van Ells.

Cover art: Silvia Rojas/Getty Images
Text composition: ElectraGraphics, Inc.
Text font: 11.5/13 Minion
Credits: See page 212.

Library of Congress Cataloging-in-Publication Data

Northstar. Listening and speaking. — 3rd ed.
    4 v. ; cm.
  Rev. ed. of: Northstar / Robin Mills and Helen Solórzano, 2nd. ed. 2004.
  The third edition of the Northstar series has been expanded to 4 separate volumes. Each level is in a separate volume with different contributing authors.
  Includes bibliographical references.
  Contents: Level 2: Basic Low Intermediate /Laurie Frazier, Robin Mills — Level 3: Intermediate / Helen Solórzano, Jennifer P.L. Schmidt — Level 4: High Intermediate / Tess Ferree, Kim Sanabria — Level 5: Advanced / Sherry Preiss.
    ISBN-13: 978-0-13-240988-9 (pbk. : student text bk. level 2 : alk. paper)
    ISBN-10: 0-13-240988-7 (pbk. : student text bk. level 2 : alk. paper)
    ISBN-13: 978-0-13-613313-1 (pbk. : student text bk. level 3 : alk. paper)
    ISBN-10: 0-13-613313-4 (pbk. : student text bk. level 3 : alk. paper)
    [etc.]
  1. English language—Textbooks for foreign speakers. 2. English language—Spoken English—Problems, exercises, etc. 3. Listening—Problems, exercises, etc. I. Mills, Robin, 1964– Northstar. II. Title: Listening and speaking.
  PE1128.N674 2008
  428.2'4—dc22

                        2008024491

ISBN 10: 0-13-240988-7
ISBN 13: 978-0-13-240988-9

Printed in the United States of America
1 2 3 4 5 6 7 8 9 10—CRK—13 12 11 10 09 08

CONTENTS

WELCOME TO NORTHSTAR
THIRD EDITION

NorthStar, now in its third edition, motivates students to succeed in their **academic** as well as **personal** language goals.

For each of the five levels, the two strands—*Reading and Writing* and *Listening and Speaking*—provide a fully integrated approach for students and teachers.

WHAT IS SPECIAL ABOUT THE THIRD EDITION?

NEW THEMES

New themes and **updated content**—presented in a **variety of genres**, including literature and lectures, and in **authentic reading and listening selections**—challenge students intellectually.

ACADEMIC SKILLS

More purposeful **integration of critical thinking** and an enhanced focus on **academic skills** such as inferencing, synthesizing, note taking, and test taking help students develop strategies for **success** in the **classroom** and on **standardized tests**. A **culminating productive task** galvanizes content, language, and **critical thinking skills**.

➤ In the *Listening and Speaking* strand, a **structured approach** gives students opportunities for **more extended and creative oral practice**, for example, presentations, simulations, debates, case studies, and public service announcements.

➤ In the *Reading and Writing* strand, a new, **fully integrated writing section** leads students through the **writing process** with engaging writing assignments focusing on various rhetorical modes.

NEW DESIGN

Full **color pages** with more **photos, illustrations, and graphic organizers** foster student engagement and make the content and activities come alive.

MyNorthStarLab

MyNorthStarLab, an easy-to-use **online learning and assessment program**, offers:

➤ Unlimited access to reading and listening selections and DVD segments.

➤ Focused test preparation to help students succeed on international exams such as TOEFL® and IELTS®. Pre- and post-unit assessments improve results by providing individualized instruction, instant feedback, and personalized study plans.

➤ Original activities that support and extend the *NorthStar* program. These include pronunciation practice using voice recording tools, and activities to build note taking skills and academic vocabulary.

➤ Tools that save time. These include a flexible gradebook and authoring features that give teachers control of content and help them track student progress.

THE NORTHSTAR APPROACH

The *NorthStar* series is based on **current research in language acquisition** and on the **experiences of teachers and curriculum designers**. Five principles guide the *NorthStar* approach.

PRINCIPLES

1 The more profoundly students are stimulated intellectually and emotionally, the more language they will use and retain.

The thematic organization of *NorthStar* promotes intellectual and emotional stimulation. The 50 sophisticated themes in *NorthStar* present intriguing topics such as recycled fashion, restorative justice, personal carbon footprints, and microfinance. The authentic content engages students, links them to language use outside of the classroom, and encourages personal expression and critical thinking.

2 Students can learn both the form and content of the language.

Grammar, vocabulary, and culture are inextricably woven into the units, providing students with systematic and multiple exposures to language forms in a variety of contexts. As the theme is developed, students can express complex thoughts using a higher level of language.

3 Successful students are active learners.

Tasks are designed to be creative, active, and varied. Topics are interesting and up-to-date. Together these tasks and topics (1) allow teachers to bring the outside world into the classroom and (2) motivate students to apply their classroom learning in the outside world.

4 Students need feedback.

This feedback comes naturally when students work together practicing language and participating in open-ended opinion and inference tasks. Whole class activities invite teachers' feedback on the spot or via audio/video recordings or notes. The innovative new MyNorthStarLab gives students immediate feedback as they complete computer-graded language activities online; it also gives students the opportunity to submit writing or speaking assignments electronically to their instructor for feedback later.

5 The quality of relationships in the language classroom is important because students are asked to express themselves on issues and ideas.

The information and activities in *NorthStar* promote genuine interaction, acceptance of differences, and authentic communication. By building skills and exploring ideas, the exercises help students participate in discussions and write essays of an increasingly complex and sophisticated nature.

THE NORTHSTAR UNIT

① FOCUS ON THE TOPIC

This section introduces students to the unifying theme of the listening selections.

> **PREDICT** and **SHARE INFORMATION** foster interest in the unit topic and help students develop a personal connection to it.
>
> **BACKGROUND** AND **VOCABULARY** activities provide students with tools for understanding the first listening selection. Later in the unit, students review this vocabulary and learn related idioms, collocations, and word forms. This helps them explore content and expand their written and spoken language.

UNIT 10

Endangered Languages

Hey, what's up?

Not much.

① FOCUS ON THE TOPIC

Ⓐ PREDICT

Look at the pictures and discuss the questions with the class.

1. What language are the people on the left speaking?
2. Do you recognize the language on the right? What is it? Do people speak it today?
3. Why do you think people stop speaking a language?

161

Ⓑ SHARE INFORMATION

Work with a partner. Discuss the questions and write your partner's answers in the chart. Then share the answers with the class.

QUESTIONS	PARTNER'S ANSWERS
1. What is your native language (first language)?	
2. How many languages do you speak?	
3. Do you speak the same language as your parents?	
4. Do you speak the same language as your grandparents?	
5. What languages do you think the children in your family will learn? Do you want them to learn a different language?	
6. What is the official language (language used by the government) of your country?	

Ⓒ BACKGROUND AND VOCABULARY

1 Read and listen to an excerpt from a textbook about endangered languages.

LANGUAGE TODAY

Language Loss

There are more than 6,000 languages in the world today. Unfortunately, many of these languages are **endangered**. An endangered language is a language that few people are learning to speak. When an endangered language loses all of its speakers, it becomes **extinct**. Sometimes a language **disappears** when the language of a more **powerful** community **replaces** it. For example, this happened when English replaced many native languages in North America. Today, many Native Americans only speak English instead of their native language.

162   UNIT 10

② FOCUS ON LISTENING

This section focuses on understanding two contrasting listening selections.

> **LISTENING ONE** is a radio report, interview, lecture, or other genre that addresses the unit topic. In levels 1 to 3, listenings are based on authentic materials. In levels 4 and 5, all the listenings are authentic.
>
> **LISTEN FOR MAIN IDEAS** and **LISTEN FOR DETAILS** are comprehension activities that lead students to an understanding and appreciation of the first selection.
>
> The **MAKE INFERENCES** activity prompts students to "listen between the lines," move beyond the literal meaning, exercise critical thinking skills, and understand the listening on a more academic level. Students follow up with pair or group work to discuss topics in the **EXPRESS OPINIONS** section.

---

② FOCUS ON LISTENING

Ⓐ LISTENING ONE: What Ever Happened to Manners?

🔊 *Listen to the beginning of the radio show called* What Ever Happened to Manners? *How do you think Sarah Jones did an international survey of manners? List three possible ways.*

1. _____
2. _____
3. _____

◀ LISTEN FOR MAIN IDEAS

🔊 *Listen to the complete interview. Then read each question and circle the correct answer.*

1. Why did Sarah Jones do a survey of manners?
   a. She wanted to see if people in one country are more polite than in other countries.
   b. She wanted to see if it is true that people are becoming very rude.
   c. She wanted to see if women are more polite than men.

2. Who did the woman test?
   a. all kinds of people
   b. students and businesspeople
   c. only students

3. What situations were included in the survey?
   a. holding the door for someone, helping someone pick up some papers, and letting someone sit down
   b. helping someone pick up some papers, helping someone cross the street, and customer service
   c. holding the door for someone, helping someone pick up some papers, and customer service

◀ LISTEN FOR DETAILS

🔊 *Listen to the interview again. Then complete the summary of the survey that Sarah Jones did.*

_____ reporters went to large cities all around the world. They went
  1.
to _____ countries. In the survey, they tested _____
     2.   3.
people. The reporters did three things: _____, the paper drop test,
                                              4.
and they looked at _____.
                        5.

For the door test, they wanted to see if people would _____ for the
                                                            6.
reporters. For the _____, they wanted to see if anyone would help
                        7.
them pick up _____. For customer service, they wanted to see if
                  8.
people who work in stores were polite: if people did courteous things like saying

_____ and _____.
     9.   10.

In the most courteous city, _____ percent of the people passed the door
                                 11.
test. When the reporters dropped their papers, only _____ percent
                                                          12.
helped pick them up. For customer service, _____ out of 20 people said
                                                 13.
"thank-you." When the reporters asked them, some people said they do it because it

shows _____. _____ was the most courteous city.
           14.   15.

◀ MAKE INFERENCES

Listen to two excerpts from the interview. After listening to each excerpt, read the question and circle the correct answer.

🔊 **Excerpt One**

Why does Sarah Jones stress the word *her*?
   a. to show the person was a woman
   b. to show that the woman needed help more than the reporter did

🔊 **Excerpt Two**

Why does Sarah Jones stress the word *are*?
   a. She agrees they are courteous because they are being paid.
   b. She thinks they have good training.

◀ EXPRESS OPINIONS

Discuss the questions with the class.

1. New York City scored as the number one city for good manners. Are you surprised? Why or why not?
2. In your opinion, are people less polite nowadays than in the past? Give examples to explain your opinion.
3. Where did you learn manners: At home? At school? At a religious institution?
4. Why are manners important?

LISTENING TWO offers another perspective on the topic and is usually another genre. Again, in levels 1 to 3, the listenings are based on authentic materials and in levels 4 and 5, they are authentic. This second listening is followed by an activity that challenges students to question ideas they formed about the first listening, and to use appropriate language skills to analyze and explain their ideas.

INTEGRATE LISTENINGS ONE AND TWO presents culminating activities. Students are challenged to take what they have learned, organize the information, and synthesize it in a meaningful way. Students practice skills that are essential for success in authentic academic settings and on standardized tests.

B **LISTENING TWO: My Life, My Language**

Listen to the class guest-speaker talk about her experience with her native language and culture. Then read each question and circle the correct answer.

1. Where does she live?
   a. New Zealand   b. Greenland
2. What language did she learn in school?
   a. Maori   b. English
3. What language did her grandparents speak?
   a. Maori   b. English
4. How did she feel in her family?
   a. empty and different   b. happy and excited
5. Where do her children learn Maori language and culture?
   a. in elementary school   b. in language nests
6. What is a language nest?
   a. a pre-school   b. a home school
7. What is / are the official language(s) of New Zealand now?
   a. English   b. English and Maori
8. What are three Maori values that children learn?
   a. love, caring, and respect for elders   b. hope, sharing, and family responsibilities
9. Who teaches the Maori adults their language and culture?
   a. linguists   b. older Maoris
10. Where do they meet?
    a. in schools   b. in neighborhood centers

Young Maori boys

C **INTEGRATE LISTENINGS ONE AND TWO**

◀ **STEP 1: Organize**

Work with a partner. In the chart, list the examples from Listening Two for each idea from Listening One.

REASONS FOR LANGUAGE LOSS	EXAMPLES FROM LISTENING TWO
1. Children don't learn the language in school.	Children only learned English, not Maori, in school.
2. Children stop learning the language and only old people speak it.	
3. Children don't learn the culture.	

WAYS TO SAVE LANGUAGES AND CULTURES
1. Children learn the language and culture.
2. The government makes the language official.
3. Adults learn the language and culture.

◀ **STEP 2: Synthesize**

Work with the same partner. Student A, you are the student asking questions; Student B, you are the professor giving examples. Begin by asking about the reasons for language loss, and then ask about ways to save languages and cultures. If the answer is not complete, ask a follow-up question, such as "Could you say more about that?" Then switch roles. Use the information from Step 1.

Example

A: Why are we losing so many languages?
B: One reason for language loss is because children don't learn their native language in school.
A: Could you say more about that?
B: Before, Maori children only learned English in school, so they couldn't speak Maori with their grandparents. Now, they learn Maori and English.

---

③ FOCUS ON SPEAKING

This section emphasizes development of productive skills for speaking. It includes sections on vocabulary, grammar, pronunciation, functional language, and an extended speaking task.

> The **VOCABULARY** section leads students from reviewing the unit vocabulary, to practicing and expanding their use of it, and then working with it—using it creatively in both this section and in the final speaking task.
>
> Students learn useful structures for speaking in the **GRAMMAR** section, which offers a concise presentation and targeted practice. Vocabulary items are recycled here, providing multiple exposures leading to mastery. For additional practice with the grammar presented, students and teachers can consult the GRAMMAR BOOK REFERENCES at the end of the book for corresponding material in the *Focus on Grammar* and Azar series.

---

③ FOCUS ON SPEAKING

Ⓐ VOCABULARY

◀ REVIEW

Read each group of four words. Circle the words that are similar to the first word in each line. Then compare your answers with a partner's. Explain why the words are similar. Explain why the other one doesn't fit.

1. amusement park	lodging	art gallery	museum
2. hotel	campsite	sleeping bag	inn
3. guest	tourist	traveler	travel agent
4. take a tour	relax on the beach	go sightseeing	go shopping
5. go hiking	go to the theater	go swimming	explore the wilderness

◀ EXPAND

1 *Read the article from a student newspaper.*

Traveling on a Budget

It's almost spring break. Are you tired of studying? Are you ready to take a trip and (1) **get away from it all**, but you don't have a lot of money? Don't worry! It's possible to travel (2) **on a budget** and still (3) **have a great time**.

One great way to see the world (4) **on a shoestring** is to (5) **go backpacking**. Just put some clothes in a backpack and you're ready to go. To save money, you can travel by bus, train, boat, or even a bicycle. For inexpensive lodging, you can choose to stay in (6) **youth hostels**. In youth hostels you can share a room with other travelers for very little money. It's also a great way to meet other travelers from different places. Traveling with another person is also a great way to have fun and save money. It will cost you less if you share the expenses of transportation, lodging, and food with a friend.

If you like to see a new place and help others at the same time, you might want to take a volunteer vacation. On a volunteer vacation, you travel to another city or country and help the people in that area. For example, you might help park rangers save the plants and animals. Or you might help people build new homes. On a volunteer vacation you really (7) **get to know** the people and place you are visiting because you usually stay with a local family and live like they do. It's not your typical vacation, but it can be a great (8) **experience**.

132   UNIT 8

Ⓑ GRAMMAR: *Can and Can't*

1 *Read the sentences. Look at the underlined words. Then answer the questions.*

What <u>can</u> you <u>do</u> at the Ice Hotel?
You <u>can look</u> at paintings in the art gallery.
You <u>can't go</u> swimming.

a. What are the verbs in each sentence? In what form is the main verb?

b. What does *can* mean? What does *can't* mean?

CAN AND CAN'T	
Can is a modal. Modals are words that come before main verbs. They change the meaning of the verbs in some way.	
1. Use *can* to talk about ability, things you are able to do.	I **can** ice skate. I took lessons last year.
Use *can't* to talk about inability.	My brother **can't** ski. He's never tried it.
2. Use *can* to talk about possibility, things that are possible.	You **can** stay at the Ice Hotel only in the winter.
Use *can't* to talk about things that are not possible.	You **can't** stay at the Ice Hotel in the summer because it isn't there.
3. *Can* and *can't* come before the main verb. The main verb is in the **base form**.	[base form] You can go ice skating in Sweden. I can't go on vacation right now.
4. Use *can* and *can't* in questions and short answers. Do not use a main verb in a short answer.	A: **Can** you swim? B: Yes, I can. A: **Can** Ellen ice skate? B: No, she **can't**.

2 *Work in a group of three. You want to find out your partners' abilities. Before you interview them, write their names in the chart on page 135. Then write five yes / no questions with can. Interview your partners and note their answers in the chart.*

Example
A: Can you dance?
B: Yes, I can.
C: No, I can't.

134   UNIT 8

The **PRONUNCIATION** section presents both controlled and freer, communicative practice of the sounds and patterns of English. Models from the listening selections reinforce content and vocabulary. This is followed by the **FUNCTION** section where students are exposed to functional language that prepares them to express ideas on a higher level. Examples have been chosen based on frequency, variety, and usefulness for the final speaking task.

The **PRODUCTION** section gives students an opportunity to integrate the ideas, vocabulary, grammar, pronunciation, and function presented in the unit. This final speaking task is the culminating activity of the unit and gets students to exchange ideas and express opinions in sustained speaking contexts. Activities are presented in a sequence that builds confidence and fluency, and allows for more than one "try" at expression. When appropriate, students practice some presentation skills: audience analysis, organization, eye contact, or use of visuals.

C SPEAKING

◖ PRONUNCIATION: Intonation: Attention Getters and Polite Questions

When we want to get someone's attention, we can say "Excuse me" or "Sorry." When we say "Sorry" to get someone's attention, we are saying, "I'm sorry if I am interrupting you, but I need to talk to you." We can also get a person's attention by saying the person's name, "Sonia," "Mr. Smith." With strangers, we can say "Sir," "Miss," or "Ma'am" (*Ma'am* / mæm / rhymes with "ham"). We use a special intonation with attention getters like "Excuse me" or "Mr. Jones."

CD 7 *Listen to the attention getters.*

Excuse me, . . .   Sir, . . .

Sorry, . . .   Mr. Smith, ...

Listen to the attention getters again. At the end of the attention getter, does the voice fall to a low note or does it stay a little high?

When we ask polite questions, we use a special intonation.

CD 7 *Listen to the questions.*

Do you have the time?

Can you hold the door for me?

Would you like me to hold the door for you?

1 CD 7 *With polite questions, the speaker's voice falls to a low note and then rises to a high note. Listen to the questions again. Underline the word(s) where the voice falls to a low note and then rises to a high note.*

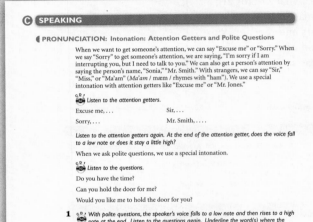

INTONATION PATTERNS	
Attention getters Your voice rises a little at the end.	Excuse me, . . . Miss, . . .
Polite questions Your voice falls to a low note on the important word and then continues to rise to a high note. The important part of the intonation pattern is the fall to the low note and then the rise to a high note.	Do you have the time? Can you hold the door for me?
Attention getters and polite questions together	Excuse me, do you have the time? Sonia, can you hold the door for me?

---

3. Student A: You are in a movie theater, watching a movie. Student B is talking to friends and it bothers you.

   Student B: You are talking to your friends during the movie.

4. Student A: You are sending text messages to another friend while Student B is trying to talk to you.

   Student B: You are trying to have a conversation with Student A.

◖ PRODUCTION: Role Play

In this activity, you will **discuss a situation, then prepare a three-to-five-minute role play that relates to manners**. A role play is a short performance. The actors take on roles, or become characters, and act out a situation. The situations are often similar to experiences that people might have in real life. Try to use the vocabulary, grammar, pronunciation, and language for making polite complaints that you learned in the unit.*

Work in a group of three. Follow the steps.

Step 1: Read each situation aloud in your group. Discuss the situations. What was rude? Why was it rude? How could you react? What could you say? What might happen if you say something?

Situations

1. You are in a restaurant having dinner with a friend. A person is sitting alone at a table near you, talking loudly on a cell phone. You can't hear your friend or enjoy your meal.

2. You are in the grocery store, standing in line to pay for your groceries. You are in a hurry to go to a friend's house. The person in line in front of you and the cashier are having a long conversation.

3. You are at the movies with a friend. It is a new movie and very popular. The line is long and you don't know if you will get tickets. Someone has been standing in line in front of you alone. Suddenly, three of his friends come and get in line in front of you and your friend.

4. You are driving with your friend. Another car comes close behind you, quickly passes, then drives very closely in front of you. A few minutes later, you stop to buy a cup of coffee. You go into the restaurant, look out the window, and see the same car stop as well. The driver comes into the restaurant.

*For Alternative Speaking Topics, see page 88.

ALTERNATIVE SPEAKING TOPICS are provided at the end of the unit. They can be used as *alternatives* to the final speaking task, or as *additional* assignments. RESEARCH TOPICS tied to the theme of the unit are organized in a special section at the back of the book.

COMPONENTS

TEACHER'S MANUAL WITH ACHIEVEMENT TESTS

Each level and strand of *NorthStar* has an accompanying Teacher's Manual with step-by-step **teaching suggestions**, including unique guidance for using *NorthStar* in secondary classes. The manuals include time guidelines, expansion activities, and techniques and instructions for using MyNorthStarLab. Also included are reproducible unit-by-unit achievement **tests** of **receptive** and **productive** skills, **answer keys** to both the student book and tests, and a unit-by-unit **vocabulary** list.

EXAMVIEW

NorthStar ExamView is a stand-alone CD-ROM that allows teachers to **create and customize** their own *NorthStar* tests.

DVD

The *NorthStar* DVD has **engaging**, **authentic video clips**, including animation, documentaries, interviews, and biographies, that correspond to the themes in *NorthStar*. Each theme contains a three- to five-minute segment that can be used with either the *Reading and Writing* strand or the *Listening and Speaking* strand. The video clips can also be viewed in MyNorthStarLab.

COMPANION WEBSITE

The companion website, www.longman.com/northstar, includes resources for teachers, such as the **scope and sequence**, **correlations** to other Longman products and to state standards, and **podcasts** from the *NorthStar* authors and series editors.

MyNorthStarLab

 **PEARSON LONGMAN** mynorthstarlab   AVAILABLE WITH the new edition of ***NORTHSTAR***

NorthStar is now available with **MyNorthStarLab**—an easy-to-use **online** program **for students and teachers** that saves time and improves results.

> ➤ **STUDENTS** receive **personalized instruction** and **practice** in all four skills. Audio, video, and test preparation are all in **one** place—available **anywhere, anytime**.

> ➤ **TEACHERS** can take advantage of many resources including online **assessments**, a flexible **gradebook**, and **tools for monitoring student progress**.

CHECK IT OUT! GO TO www.mynorthstarlab.com FOR A PREVIEW!

TURN THE PAGE TO SEE KEY FEATURES OF **MyNorthStarLab**.

MyNorthStarLab

MyNorthStarLab supports students with **individualized instruction,
feedback,** and **extra help.** A wide array of resources, including a flexible
gradebook, helps teachers manage student progress.

The MyNorthStarLab **WELCOME** page **organizes assignments and grades,** and **facilitates communication** between students and teachers.

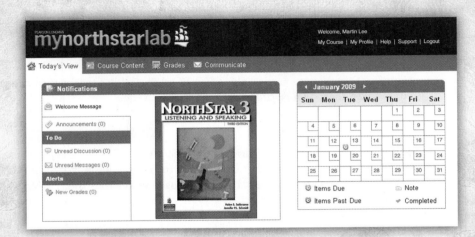

For each unit, MyNorthStarLab provides a **READINESS CHECK.**

➤ Activities **assess** student knowledge **before** beginning the unit and **follow up** with individualized instruction.

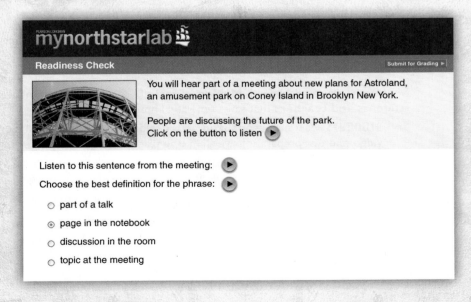

Student book material and **new** practice activities are available to students online.

➤ Students benefit from virtually unlimited **practice anywhere, anytime**.

Interaction with **Internet** and **video** materials will:

➤ Expand students' knowledge of the topic.

➤ Help students practice new vocabulary and grammar.

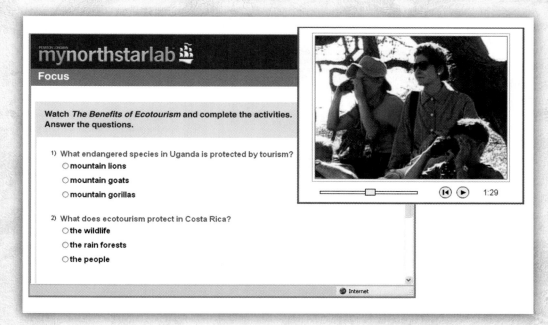

INTEGRATED SKILL ACTIVITIES in MyNorthStarLab challenge students to bring together the **language skills** and **critical thinking skills** that they have practiced throughout the unit.

Integrated Task - Read, Listen, Write   Submit for Grading ▶

THE ADVENTURE OF A LIFETIME

We at the Antarctic Travel Society <u>encourage</u> you to consider an excited guided tour of Antarctica for your next vacation.

The Antarctic Travel society carefully plans and operates tours of the Antarctic by ship. There are three trips per day leaving from <u>ports</u> in South America and Australia. Each ship carries only about 100 passengers at a time. Tours run from November through March to the ice-free areas along the coast of Antarctica.

In addition to touring the coast, our ships stop for on-land visits, which generally last for about three hours. Activities include guided sightseeing, mountain climbing, camping, <u>kayaking</u>, and <u>scuba diving</u>. For a longer stay, camping trips can also be arranged.

Our tours will give you an opportunity to experience the richness of Antarctica, including its wildlife, history, active research stations, and, most of all, its natural beauty.

Tours are <u>supervised</u> by the ship's staff. The staff generally includes <u>experts</u> in animal and sea life and other Antarctica specialists. There is generally one staff member for every 10 to 20 passengers. Theses trained and responsible individuals will help to make your visit to Antarctica safe, educational, and <u>unforgettable</u>.

READ, LISTEN AND WRITE ABOUT TOURISM IN ANTARCTICA
Read.
Read the text. Then answer the question.

According to the text, how can tourism benefit the Antartic?

▶ **Listen.**
Click on the Play button and listen to the passage.
Use the outline to take notes as you listen.

Main idea:

Seven things that scientists study:

The effects of tourism:

Write.
Write about the potential and risks in Antarctica.
Follow the steps to prepare.

Step 1
• Review the text and your outline from the listening task.
• Write notes about the benefits and risks of tourism.

Step 2
Write for 20 minutes. Leave 5 minutes to edit your work.

The MyNorthStarLab **ASSESSMENT** tools allow instructors to customize and deliver achievement tests online.

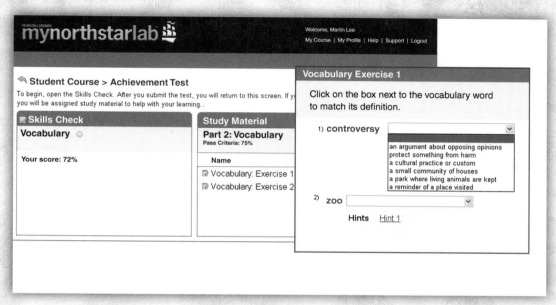

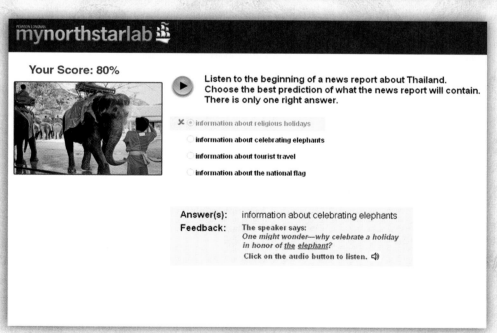

SCOPE AND SEQUENCE

UNIT	CRITICAL THINKING	LISTENING
1 **Offbeat Jobs** **Theme:** Work **Listening One:** *What's My Job?* An excerpt from a game show **Listening Two:** *More Offbeat Jobs* A conversation	Classify information Rank personal values and preferences in work Relate personal skills to job responsibilities Infer word meaning from context Infer situational context Support opinions with information from the interviews Interpret illustrations	Predict content Listen for main ideas Listen for details Interpret speakers' attitudes Sort information from the interview Relate listenings to personal experience Organize and synthesize information from the listenings
2 **Building a Better Community** **Theme:** The Country and the City **Listening One:** *A New-Urbanist Community* A radio interview **Listening Two:** *Let's Hear from Our Listeners* A call-in portion of the radio show	Analyze photographs Evaluate the advantages and disadvantages of different living environments Interpret bar graphs and maps Infer information not explicit in a text Infer word meaning from context Redesign a neighborhood	Predict content Listen for main ideas Listen for details Interpret speaker's tone and attitude Identify contrasting viewpoints Relate listenings to personal opinions Organize and synthesize information from the listenings
3 **A Penny Saved is a Penny Earned** **Theme:** Money **Listening One:** *A Barter Network* A community meeting **Listening Two:** *The Compact* A conversation	Interpret a cartoon Assess personal consumer habits Interpret a timeline Compare and contrast monetary and bartering systems Infer word meaning from context Organize information into a web diagram Evaluate consumer behavior Categorize goods and services	Predict content Listen for main ideas Listen for details Interpret speaker's tone and emotions Relate listenings to personal experiences Organize and synthesize information from the listenings
4 **Innocent or Guilty?** **Theme:** Criminal justice **Listening One:** *Roger's Story* A personal story **Listening Two:** *Why Do Innocent People Go to Prison?* A radio interview	Interpret an illustration Analyze eyewitness testimony Formulate and support a moral position Infer word meaning from context Classify information as general statements or examples Prioritize items based on an array of criteria	Predict content Listen for main ideas Listen for details Infer speakers' attitudes Relate listenings to personal experiences Organize and synthesize information from the listenings

SPEAKING	VOCABULARY	GRAMMAR	PRONUNCIATION
Express and defend opinions Act out a conversation Make small talk Interview a classmate Talk about skills and characteristics Assess classmates' skills and recommend a job	Use context clues to find meaning Define words Use expressions for small talk	Descriptive adjectives	Stress patterns of nouns and adjectives
Discuss and find locations on a map Classify negative and positive information Share opinions Express agreement Talk about your community Interview classmates about neighborhood preferences Discuss costs and benefits of different neighborhood designs Present a redesigned neighborhood	Use context clues to find meaning Define words Demonstrate vocabulary usage	*This/That/These/Those* and *One*	TH sounds
Share opinions and experiences Practice bartering for goods and services Use new vocabulary in conversation Make suggestions and come to an agreement Compare products and services	Use context clues to find meaning Define words Use idiomatic expressions and synonyms	Comparative adjectives	Numbers and prices
Make predictions Share opinions and experiences Describe a drawing in detail Conduct an interview Express and support opinions Role-play a conversation Negotiate with classmates to reach agreement	Use context clues to find meaning Define words	Simple past: *yes / no* questions and *wh-* questions	*-ed* endings—a sound or a syllable?

SCOPE AND SEQUENCE

UNIT	CRITICAL THINKING	LISTENING
5 Etiquette **Theme:** Etiquette **Listening One:** *What Ever Happened to Manners?* A radio interview **Listening Two:** *Our Listeners Respond— Why is There a Lack of Manners?* A call-in portion of the radio show	Interpret an illustration Rank personal opinions about manners and certain behaviors Summarize and analyze responses Infer information not explicit in a text Infer word meaning from context Classify information Propose solutions	Predict content Listen for main ideas Listen for details Interpret speaker's tone and attitude Organize and synthesize information from the listenings Listen for sentence level intonation Listen to and take notes on students' role plays
6 Who's Game for These Games? **Theme:** Games **Listening One:** *Entertainment for All* A news broadcast **Listening Two:** *Do You Like Video Games, Too?* A conversation	Analyze photographs Rank personal opinions about games Interpret pie charts Infer information not explicit in a text Infer word meaning from context Formulate and defend a position on the value of electronic games	Predict content Listen for main ideas Listen for and categorize supporting details Infer speakers' meaning Relate listening to personal experiences Organize and synthesize information from the listenings Listen for word linking Listen to student arguments and formulate counterarguments
7 Good-Mood Foods **Theme:** Food **Listening One:** *Street Talk* An excerpt from a radio show **Listening Two:** *What's the Matter?* Three excerpts from a radio show	Identify personal attitudes toward food Interpret a chart Infer word meaning from context Categorize collocations Propose food solutions Design a restaurant Interpret illustrations	Predict content Listen for main ideas Listen for and identify details Infer speaker's tone and reaction Relate listening to personal experiences Listen and take notes using a chart Organize and synthesize information from the listenings Compare and contrast sounds

SPEAKING	VOCABULARY	GRAMMAR	PRONUNCIATION
Express opinions Complain politely Talk about etiquette Interview classmates Role-play situations Debate the rudeness of certain behaviors	Use context clues to find meaning Define words Use idiomatic expressions	*Could* and *would* in polite questions	Intonation: attention getters and polite questions
Discuss information from charts Share opinions Disagree politely and offer different opinions Play a word game Interview classmates Debate the value of video games	Use context clues to find meaning Define words Use idiomatic expressions	Adverbs and expressions of frequency	Joining words together
Make predictions Describe illustrations Express opinions Compare and discuss solutions Politely make suggestions Politely accept or refuse suggestions Role-play Present a restaurant design and menu to the class	Use context clues to find meaning Use collocations Use phrasal verbs	Count and non-count nouns	Vowels [ʊ] and [uw]

SCOPE AND SEQUENCE

UNIT	CRITICAL THINKING	LISTENING

8 **An Ice Place to Stay**
 	
Theme: Travel
Listening One: *An Unusual Vacation*
  A telephone conversation
Listening Two: *Vacations around the World*
  A recording describing three vacation spots
	Interpret a photograph
	Rank personal preferences in travel
	Categorize information
	Evaluate vacation places according to criteria
		Predict content
		Listen for main ideas
		Listen for details
		Infer speaker's tone and attitude
		Organize and synthesize information from the listenings
		Take notes
		Compare and contrast sounds

9 **Staying Healthy**
 	
Theme: Health problems and treatments
Listening One: *Thin Fast*
  A radio commercial
Listening Two: *Being Healthy is Good for You!*
  A conversation
	Interpret a cartoon
	Assess and categorize personal health practices
	Infer word meaning from context
	Classify health factors
	Analyze common health problems and prevention strategies
		Predict content
		Listen for main ideas
		Listen for details
		Evaluate speakers' opinions
		Take notes
		Organize and synthesize information from the listenings
		Distinguish sounds

10 **Endangered Languages**
 	
Theme: Languages
Listening One: *Language Loss*
  A lecture
Listening Two: *My Life, My Language*
  An autobiographical account
	Interpret photographs
	Infer information not explicit in a text
	Infer word meaning from context
	Hypothesize reasons
	Support opinions with reasons
	Correlate specific examples to broad themes
	Summarize and evaluate classmates' findings
		Predict content
		Listen for main ideas
		Listen for details
		Infer speaker's tone and attitude
		Organize and synthesize information from the listenings
		Relate listening to personal opinions

SPEAKING	VOCABULARY	GRAMMAR	PRONUNCIATION
Express opinions Make polite requests Role-play a conversation Survey classmates Discuss vacation options Talk about travel Express likes and dislikes	Use context clues to find meaning Define words Use idiomatic expressions and synonyms	*Can* and *can't*	*Can* and *can't*
Express opinions Express concern about health problems Give and receive advice about health problems Discuss health practices Interview people about health practices Role-play a public service announcement	Use context clues to find meaning Define words Identify synonyms	*Should, ought to,* and *have to*	Reductions: *hafta, hasta, oughta*
Share personal history Express opinions Survey classmates Role-play situations about language learning Talk about preserving languages Report findings on endangered languages Make predictions and suggestions	Use context clues to find meaning Define words Use idiomatic expressions	Future with *will, may,* and *might*	Using contractions with *will*

ACKNOWLEDGMENTS

We would like to express our appreciation to the many people who helped make this book possible. Thanks go to Frances Boyd and Carol Numrich who helped to guide and shape our many ideas into the final text. Many thanks go to Debbie Sistino for her skillful management of this project and to Gosia Jaros-White, whose suggestions and careful editing were invaluable to us.

We would also like to thank our family and friends who offered their support and input. In particular, we thank Stefan Frazier, Jackie LeDoux and Caroline LeDoux for contributing their feedback and insights into the world of gaming; and Jyotirmoy Saha for sharing his knowledge of Mumbai and Indian culture. Thanks also to Jonathan Livingston for being a good sounding board and all-around great companion.

Laurie Frazier
Robin Mills

Reviewers

For the comments and insights they graciously offered to help shape the direction of the Third Edition of *NorthStar*, the publisher would like to thank the following reviewers and institutions.

Gail August, Hostos Community College; **Anne Bachmann**, Clackamas Community College; **Aegina Barnes**, York College, CUNY; **Dr. Sabri Bebawi**, San Jose Community College; **Kristina Beckman**, John Jay College; **Jeff Bellucci**, Kaplan Boston; **Nathan Blesse**, Human International Academy; **Alan Brandman**, Queens College; **Laila Cadavona-Dellapasqua**, Kaplan; **Amy Cain**, Kaplan; **Nigel Caplan**, Michigan State University; **Alzira Carvalho**, Human International Academy, San Diego; **Chao-Hsun (Richard) Cheng**, Wenzao Ursuline College of Languages; **Mu-hua (Yolanda) Chi**, Wenzao Ursuline College of Languages; **Liane Cismowski**, Olympic High School; **Shauna Croft**, MESLS; **Misty Crooks**, Kaplan; **Amanda De Loera**, Kaplan English Programs; **Jennifer Dobbins**, New England School of English; **Luis Dominguez**, Angloamericano; **Luydmila Drgaushanskaya**, ASA College; **Dilip Dutt**, Roxbury Community College; **Christie Evenson**, Chung Dahm Institute; **Patricia Frenz-Belkin**, Hostos Community College, CUNY; **Christiane Galvani**, Texas Southern University; **Joanna Ghosh**, University of Pennsylvania; **Cristina Gomes**, Kaplan Test Prep; **Kristen Grinager**, Lincoln High School; **Janet Harclerode**, Santa Monica College; **Carrell Harden**, HCCS, Gulfton Campus; **Connie Harney**, Antelope Valley College; **Ann Hilborn**, ESL Consultant in Houston; **Barbara Hockman**, City College of San Francisco; **Margaret Hodgson**, NorQuest College; **Paul Hong**, Chung Dahm Institute; **Wonki Hong**, Chung Dahm Institute; **John House**, Iowa State University; **Polly Howlett**, Saint Michael's College; **Arthur Hui**, Fullerton College; **Nina Ito**, CSU, Long Beach; **Scott Jenison**, Antelope Valley College; **Hyunsook Jeong**, Keimyung University; **Mandy Kama**, Georgetown University; **Dale Kim**, Chung Dahm Institute; **Taeyoung Kim**, Keimyung University; **Woo-hyung Kim**, Keimyung University; **Young Kim**, Chung Dahm Institute; **Yu-kyung Kim**, Sunchon National University; **John Kostovich**, Miami Dade College; **Albert Kowun**, Fairfax, VA; **David Krise**, Michigan State University; **Cheri (Young Hee) Lee**, ReadingTownUSA English Language Institute; **Eun-Kyung Lee**, Chung Dahm Institute; **Sang Hyock Lee**, Keimyung University; **Debra Levitt**, SMC; **Karen Lewis**, Somerville, MA; **Chia-Hui Liu**, Wenzao Ursuline College of Languages; **Gennell Lockwood**, Seattle, WA; **Javier Lopez Anguiano**, Colegio Anglo Mexicano de Coyoacan; **Mary March**, Shoreline Community College; **Susan Matson**, ELS Language Centers; **Ralph McClain**, Embassy CES Boston; **Veronica McCormack**, Roxbury Community College; **Jennifer McCoy**, Kaplan; **Joseph McHugh**, Kaplan; **Cynthia McKeag Tsukamoto**, Oakton Community College; **Paola Medina**, Texas Southern University; **Christine Kyung-ah Moon**, Seoul, Korea; **Margaret Moore**, North Seattle Community College; **Michelle Moore**, Madison English as a Second Language School; **David Motta**, Miami University; **Suzanne Munro**, Clackamas Community College; **Elena Nehrbecki**, Hudson County CC; **Kim Newcomer**, University of Washington; **Melody Nightingale**, Santa Monica College; **Patrick Northover**, Kaplan Test and Prep; **Sarah Oettle**, Kaplan, Sacramento; **Shirley Ono**, Oakton Community College; **Maria Estela Ortiz Torres**, C. Anglo Mexicano de Coyoac'an; **Suzanne Overstreet**, West Valley College; **Linda Ozarow**, West Orange High School; **Ileana Porges-West**, Miami Dade College, Hialeah Campus; **Megan Power**, ILCSA; **Alison Robertson**, Cypress College; **Ma. Del Carmen Romero**, Universidad del Valle de Mexico; **Nina Rosen**, Santa Rosa Junior College; **Daniellah Salario**, Kaplan; **Joel Samuels**, Kaplan New York City; **Babi Sarapata**, Columbia University ALP; **Donna Schaeffer**, University of Washington; **Lynn Schneider**, City College of San Francisco; **Errol Selkirk**, New School University; **Amity Shook**, Chung Dahm Institute; **Lynn Stafford-Yilmaz**, Bellevue Community College; **Lynne Ruelaine Stokes**, Michigan State University; **Henna Suh**, Chung Dahm Institute; **Sheri Summers**, Kaplan Test Prep; **Martha Sutter**, Kent State University; **Becky Tarver Chase**, MESLS; **Lisa Waite-Trago**, Michigan State University; **Carol Troy**, Da-Yeh University; **Luci Tyrell**, Embassy CES Fort Lauderdale; **Yong-Hee Uhm**, Myongii University; **Debra Un**, New York University; **José Vazquez**, The University of Texas Pan American; **Hollyahna Vettori**, Santa Rosa Junior College; **Susan Vik**, Boston University; **Sandy Wagner**, Fort Lauderdale High School; **Joanne Wan**, ASC English; **Pat Wiggins**, Clackamas Community College; **Heather Williams**, University of Pennsylvania; **Carol Wilson-Duffy**, Michigan State University; **Kailin Yang**, Kaohsing Medical University; **Ellen Yaniv**, Boston University; **Samantha Young**, Kaplan Boston; **Yu-san Yu**, National Sun Yat-sen University; **Ann Zaaijer**, West Orange High School

UNIT 1

Offbeat Jobs

①FOCUS ON THE TOPIC

A PREDICT

Look at the pictures and discuss the questions with the class.

1. What is each person doing?

2. Which of these jobs are ordinary? Which are unusual?

3. Read the title of the unit. *Offbeat* means unusual. Can you think of any other offbeat jobs?

1

B SHARE INFORMATION

Look at the list of things to consider when choosing a job. Number the items in order of importance from 1 to 7. Number 1 is the most important and number 7 is the least important.

_____ **salary** (how much money you make)

_____ **hours** (what hours you work)

_____ **safety** (how safe or dangerous the work is)

_____ **workplace** (indoors, outdoors, home, office)

_____ **interest** (how much you like the work)

_____ **education** (how much schooling you need for the job)

_____ **number of job openings** (how easy it is to find a job)

Now work in a small group. Compare your answers. Tell why each item is important or not important to you.

Examples

Salary is important to me because I need to make money for my family.

Workplace isn't important to me because I can work anywhere—indoors, outdoors, at home, or in an office.

C BACKGROUND AND VOCABULARY

1 *Read and listen to the information on different jobs available for college students.*

Looking for a fun summer job? Need to earn some extra income? Here are some jobs you might like. Call the Career Center at 555-1111 if you want more information about these jobs.

Mountain Climbing Guide	Computer Assembler	Insurance Salesperson
Do you like exciting and sometimes dangerous activities? Do you like to work outdoors? Are you athletic? Then this is the right job for you! If you like doing unusual things, this **offbeat** job is just for you.	Do you like computers? Do you know a lot about them? We need people to work in our **factory** to make computers. You must be fast and like to build things.	Do you like sales? Do you like to work with people? Come work in our insurance company. We sell every kind of **insurance policy**: auto, home, life, and medical.

Cartoon Artist

Do you like to draw? Can you draw funny pictures? If you are artistic and **creative**, this is the right job for you.

Restaurant Reviewer

Do you like to eat in restaurants? Do you have good **taste buds** so you can **taste** many flavors? Do you like different kinds of foods like **spicy food** (Thai or Mexican) and **flavors** (sweet or sour)? If so, this is the job for you!

Game Show Contestant

Do you want to be on TV? We need **contestants** on our game show called *What's My Job?* The **host** asks you questions about jobs. The winner is the person who answers the most questions correctly.

2 *Match the words on the left with the definitions on the right.*

___c___ **1.** offbeat

_____ **2.** factory

_____ **3.** insurance policy

_____ **4.** creative

_____ **5.** taste buds

_____ **6.** taste

_____ **7.** spicy food

_____ **8.** flavor

_____ **9.** contestant

_____ **10.** host

a. thinking of new ways of doing things

b. an agreement with an insurance company to be paid money in case of an accident, illness, or death

c. different or unusual

d. someone who plays a game

e. a building where things are made

f. someone who talks to guests on a radio or TV program

g. particular taste of a food or drink

h. food with a strong flavor

i. try food by eating a little bit

j. the parts of the tongue that can taste food

②FOCUS ON LISTENING

A LISTENING ONE: What's My Job?

1 CD₇ *Listen to the beginning of* What's My Job? *Circle the correct answer to complete each statement.*

1. You are listening to a _____.

   a. job interview   **b.** game show   **c.** radio show

2. Wayne is a _____.

   a. host   **b.** contestant   **c.** guest

3. Rita is a _____.

    a. host   **b.** contestant   **c.** guest

4. Peter is going to describe _____.

    a. his job   **b.** his company   **c.** himself

2 *Make predictions. Circle more than one answer.*

Peter will talk about . . .

    a. what he does.   **c.** how much money he makes.   **e.** what he likes to do.

    b. where he works.   **d.** what he is like.

◖ LISTEN FOR MAIN IDEAS

CD 1
④ *Listen to* What's My Job? *Circle the correct answer to complete each statement.*

1. Rita asks Peter questions to guess _____.

    a. his last name   **b.** his job   **c.** his age

2. Peter works in a _____.

    a. restaurant   **b.** factory   **c.** bakery

3. Peter is _____.

    a. a factory worker   **b.** a chef   **c.** an ice-cream taster

4. Peter has to be careful with _____.

    a. his taste buds   **b.** the ice cream   **c.** the factory machines

5. Peter thinks his job is _____.

    a. tiring   **b.** great   **c.** dangerous

◖ LISTEN FOR DETAILS

CD 1
⑤ *Listen to* What's My Job? *again. Then read each statement. Write* **T** *(true) or* **F** *(false).*

_____ **1.** Peter can be creative at work.

_____ **2.** Peter thinks of new ice-cream flavors.

_____ **3.** He eats all the ice cream at work.

_____ **4.** He doesn't eat spicy foods.

_____ **5.** He doesn't drink alcohol or coffee.

_____ **6.** He smokes.

_____ **7.** He has a one-million-dollar insurance policy for his taste buds.

_____ **8.** He studied ice-cream tasting in school.

Now go back to Section 2A, Exercise 2 above. Were your predictions correct?

◖ MAKE INFERENCES

Listen to three excerpts from *What's My Job?* *After listening to each excerpt, read the statements. Circle* **True** *or* **False**.

Excerpt One

1. Wayne thinks ice-cream tasting is a difficult job.	True	False
2. Peter loves his job.	True	False

Excerpt Two

1. Wayne doesn't think Peter has to be careful.	True	False
2. Wayne is surprised that Peter can't smoke or drink alcohol.	True	False

Excerpt Three

1. Wayne doesn't think Peter went to an ice-cream tasting school.	True	False
2. Peter learned about ice-cream tasting from his family.	True	False

Compare your answers with a classmate's. Explain your answers using details from the listening.

◖ EXPRESS OPINIONS

Discuss the questions with the class. Give your opinions.

1. Do you think Peter's job is difficult or easy? Why do you think so?

2. Do you think you could do Peter's job? Why or why not?

3. Do you think it was easy for Peter to get started in his job? Why or why not?

B ⬤ LISTENING TWO: More Offbeat Jobs

1 *Look at the pictures. Where does each person work? What job is each person doing? Write the name of the job under the picture.*

_____   _____

2 CD 7 *Listen to two people talking with a job counselor about their jobs. A job counselor is someone who helps people find the right job or career.*

Look at the statements in the chart. Put a check (✓) in the correct column for the window washer or the professional shopper. Some statements may be true for both.

	WINDOW WASHER	PROFESSIONAL SHOPPER
a. I like my job.		
b. I work outdoors.		
c. I earn a high salary.		
d. My work is dangerous.		
e. I like to work with people.		
f. I'm good with money.		
g. I'm good with my hands.		
h. My work is tiring.		
i. It was difficult to get started in this job.		
j. I have my own business.		
k. I want to quit and find a new job.		
l. I don't want to be the boss.		
m. I like working for myself.		

◀ **STEP 1: Organize**

Read the questions a person might ask about these three unusual jobs. Then answer the questions with the information from Listenings One and Two.

	WINDOW WASHER	PROFESSIONAL SHOPPER	ICE-CREAM TASTER
1. Can you describe what you do?	I wash office building windows.		
2. What do you like about your job?		I love to shop.	
3. What do you dislike about your job?			
4. What's difficult about your job?			
5. What skills do you need to do your job?			

Compare your answers with a partner's. Discuss any differences.

◀ **STEP 2: Synthesize**

Work with a partner. Student A, you are a host on a radio show. You are interviewing people about their unusual jobs. Student B, you are a guest on the show. You are talking about your offbeat job. Use the questions and the information from Step 1 to guide your conversation.

Example

A: What is your job?
B: I'm a window washer.
A: Can you describe what you do?
B: I wash office building windows. I go high up in a basket to reach the windows.

Switch roles and talk about a different job from Step 1.

A VOCABULARY

◀ REVIEW

Match the statement on the left with the best response on the right.

___i___ **1.** I want to find a new job. I like my work, but I don't like being in an office. I don't want to be in a building all day.

_____ **2.** A friend of mine just got a job as a game-show host. I've never known a game-show host before.

_____ **3.** I'm so excited because I just got the job I wanted. Over forty people were trying to get that job! I knew it was the perfect job for me!

_____ **4.** I don't think I would like to work in a factory. You have to watch your work very closely so you don't make mistakes or get hurt.

_____ **5.** I would like to work as an ice-cream taster, but I'm not sure how to find that kind of work.

_____ **6.** I don't like my job. I want to get a new job.

_____ **7.** I could not be a window washer. I'm too scared to be high up on a building.

_____ **8.** I can't believe how much money basketball players make. I wish I had that much money!

_____ **9.** I love making up stories. Someday I want to write my own book.

_____ **10.** I want to be a doctor. I know I need to be in school for a long time, but being a doctor is my dream.

_____ **11.** I want to be a professional shopper because I don't want to have a boss.

_____ **12.** I think walking dogs for a job is fun. The only problem is that all the walking is a lot of work!

a. It sounds like you want to **quit**!

b. Congratulations! It sounds like it's **the right job for you**!

c. It *is* hard to **get started** in that job. Maybe you can ask a job counselor for help?

d. So, you want a **safe** job on the ground.

e. That's an **offbeat** job!

f. They *do* earn **a high salary**!

g. You are very **creative**.

h. I agree. I think it's a **dangerous** job.

i. You want to work **outdoors** then?

j. I want to **work for myself**, too.

k. If that's really what you want to do, I think it's a **career** you will enjoy.

l. Yes, it is a very **tiring** job.

Work with a partner. Read the sentences below. Circle the best definition for each word or phrase.

1. I work 60 hours a week and I always think about my work. I am a <u>workaholic</u>.

   A workaholic is a person who _____.
   - **a.** works a lot and finds it difficult not to work
   - **b.** knows a lot of people

2. I want a career where I can work with money. I am very <u>good with numbers</u>.

   Someone who is good with numbers _____.
   - **a.** likes to count and do math
   - **b.** doesn't like doing math

3. I work hard to be successful. I'm unhappy when I don't complete everything. People sometimes say I try to do too much. They call me an <u>overachiever</u>.

   An overachiever _____.
   - **a.** is usually not very busy
   - **b.** is very active and does a lot all the time

4. Some people like office jobs. Not me. I enjoy a job that lets me make things. I am <u>good with my hands</u>.

   A person who is good with his or her hands _____.
   - **a.** likes to do office work all day
   - **b.** is good at fixing or building things

5. I'm good at finding solutions to difficult situations. My friends often ask me to help them. They say I am a good <u>problem solver</u>.

   A problem solver _____.
   - **a.** is good at finding the best way to do something
   - **b.** needs a lot of help doing things

6. I really enjoy working in a store because I like talking to and helping people. I have <u>good people skills</u>.

   Someone with good people skills _____.
   - **a.** can relate well with other people
   - **b.** is usually very shy

7. I am good at telling people what I think and I can explain things well. I am very clear when I speak. I am a <u>good communicator</u>.

   A good communicator _____.
   - **a.** is difficult to understand
   - **b.** is very easy to understand

(continued on next page)

8. I always come to work on time and do my work well. Sometimes I stay longer at work to finish my job. My boss says I'm <u>hardworking</u>.

A hardworking person _____.

a. works a lot and is not lazy   **b.** doesn't do a good job

9. My favorite job was working in a restaurant. There were many people working there and we worked well together. We were all <u>team players</u>.

A team player _____.

a. works alone and doesn't help others   **b.** works in a group and helps others

10. I worked in a store last year. The boss let me count the money at the end of the day and take it to the bank. My boss didn't worry because I am <u>trustworthy</u>.

A trustworthy person is _____.

a. honest   **b.** not honest

◖ CREATE

It is a good idea to practice answering questions before you go to a job interview. Work with a partner. Practice asking and answering the questions. Use the words from the box and vocabulary from Review and Expand in your answers.

Skills: Talents or Abilities	**Characteristics: A Description of You as a Person**	**Strengths and Weaknesses:**
good with numbers	creative	good communicator
good with my hands	hardworking	problem solver
good people skills	trustworthy	overachiever
	a team player	workaholic

1. Tell me about yourself. What things do you like to do? Give an example.

I am _____

I like to _____

2. What skills do you have? Give an example of when you used that skill.

I am _____

I _____

3. What are your strengths? Give an example.

I am _____

I _____

4. What are your weaknesses? Give an example.

I am _____

I _____

B GRAMMAR: Descriptive Adjectives

1 *Work with a partner. Read the conversations aloud. Look at the underlined words. Then answer the questions.*

1. **A:** What's your job like?
   B: My job is <u>interesting</u>.

2. **A:** What kind of person are you?
   B: I'm a <u>friendly</u> person.

a. Look at the answers to the questions. What is the verb in each sentence?

b. What is the noun in each sentence?

c. Which words describe the nouns? Where do they come in the sentences?

DESCRIPTIVE ADJECTIVES	
Adjectives describe nouns. **1.** Adjectives can come after the verb **be**.	My job **is tiring**.
2. Adjectives can also come before a noun.	Artists are **creative people**.
3. When a singular noun follows an adjective, use **a** before the adjective if the adjective begins with a consonant sound.	This isn't **a high-salary job**.
4. When a singular noun follows an adjective, use **an** before the adjective if the adjective begins with a vowel sound.	Peter has **an unusual job**.

2 *Work with a partner. Take turns making statements using the nouns and adjectives provided. After one of you makes a statement, the other one reacts, saying, "I agree" or "I don't agree." If you don't agree with a statement, correct it.*

Example

a secretary's work / dangerous

A: A secretary's work is dangerous.
B: I don't agree. A secretary's work isn't dangerous. It's safe.

1. a mountain-climbing guide's job / tiring

2. an ice-cream taster / creative person

3. a basketball player's work / difficult

4. a cartoon artist /offbeat job

5. a window washer / interesting job

6. a game-show host / boring job

7. a professional shopper's job / relaxing

C SPEAKING

◖ PRONUNCIATION: Stress

In words with multiple syllables, one syllable is stressed. Stressed syllables sound longer than unstressed syllables. They are also louder and higher in pitch than unstressed syllables.

c D ɪ
🔟 *Listen to the examples.*

care<u>ful</u>

cre<u>a</u>tive

rel<u>ax</u>ing

A compound noun is formed when two nouns are used together as one noun. In compound nouns, the stress is stronger on the first word in the compound.

CD 7
🔟 *Listen to the examples.*

<u>an</u>imal trainer

<u>sales</u>clerk

When an adjective is followed by a noun, the stress is usually stronger on the noun.

CD 7
🔟 *Listen to the examples.*

professional <u>shop</u>per

good <u>pay</u>

1 **CD 7** **⓫** *Listen to the adjectives. Write the number of syllables you hear in each adjective. Then listen again and underline the stressed syllable. Listen again and repeat the words.*

_____ **1.** dangerous

_____ **2.** important

_____ **3.** tiring

_____ **4.** educated

_____ **5.** difficult

_____ **6.** spicy

_____ **7.** unusual

_____ **8.** interesting

2 **CD 7** **⓬** *Read each item and underline the stressed syllable. Listen and check your answers. Then work with a partner. Take turns saying each item and listening for the correct stress.*

_____ **1.** cartoon artist

_____ **2.** window washer

_____ **3.** high salary

_____ **4.** taste buds

_____ **5.** ice cream

_____ **6.** spicy foods

_____ **7.** department store

3 Work with a partner. Student A, ask Wh- questions with the phrases on the left. Student B, answer with the phrases on the right. Be sure to use the correct stress. Switch roles after item 4. Write your answers on the lines.

Example

A: What do you call someone who washes windows?
B: A window washer.

_b_	1. someone who washes windows
_____	2. a frozen dessert
_____	3. someone who sells things
_____	4. someone who draws cartoons
_____	5. a large store that sells many different products
_____	6. someone who puts together computers
_____	7. the parts of the tongue you use to taste food
_____	8. someone who helps people find the right job or career

a. taste buds
b. window washer
c. job counselor
d. cartoon artist
e. ice cream
f. department store
g. computer assembler
h. salesclerk

◖**FUNCTION: Small Talk**

When making conversation, it's polite to ask about a person's job and interests (what people like to do in their free time). It's also polite to express interest (to react positively) when people tell you something about themselves.

ASKING ABOUT SOMEONE'S JOB AND INTERESTS	TALKING ABOUT YOURSELF	SHOWING INTEREST
What do you do?	I'm not working right now. I'm a (student / chef / homemaker). I'm retired.[1]	Oh . . . Really?
How do you like it?	It's great. It's interesting. It's all right, but . . . I don't like it at all.	Good for you. Oh, I see. Oh, why not?
What do you like to do in your free time?	I like to (listen to music / play tennis). I enjoy (reading / playing computer games).	That's interesting. That's nice.

---

[1]**retired:** no longer working at a job, usually because of age

Work with a partner. Complete the conversation with your own information. Then practice it aloud.

A: Hi. My name's _____.

B: Hi. I'm _____. Nice to meet you.

A: Nice to meet you, too. So what do you do?

B: I'm _____.

A: _____. How do you like it?

B: _____. How about you? What do you do?

A: _____.

B: _____. So what do you like to do in your free time?

A: _____. How about you?

B: _____.

◀ **PRODUCTION: Participating in a Workshop**

> In this activity, you will **take part in a workshop for people looking for jobs.** In this workshop, people with offbeat jobs want to get different jobs. Job counselors talk with them to identify their skills and think of new jobs. Try to use the vocabulary, grammar, pronunciation, and language to make small talk that you learned in the unit.*

Follow the steps.

Step 1: Divide into two groups with an equal number of students.
Group A: people with offbeat jobs who want to change jobs
Group B: job counselors, who can help identify skills and new jobs

Group A: Each student chooses one job from the list below or another offbeat job. This is the job you now have. List the skills, characteristics, and strengths a person needs to do that job. Use words like: *creative, good with numbers,* and *trustworthy.* Then list reasons why you want to find a new job.

restaurant reviewer	ice-cream taster
cartoon artist	professional shopper
game-show host	other: _____
window washer	

---
*For Alternative Speaking Topics, see page 16.

Group B: Write five questions to ask the job holders.

Examples

What are your responsibilities?

Why do you want to change jobs?

Step 2: Form new groups of eight people—four from Group A and four from Group B. Offbeat job holders (Group A) sit in a line facing the job counselors (Group B).

Conduct a workshop:

- Each job holder briefly introduces himself or herself and then gives a short talk about his or her current job.
- Each counselor asks one or two questions to *each* job holder.

Step 3: To end the workshop, *each* job counselor names a new job that is good for the job holders. Explain which skills the job holders can use in the new jobs.

ALTERNATIVE SPEAKING TOPICS

Work in a small group. Discuss the questions.

1. Why do you think some people like offbeat jobs?
2. How do you think people get started in their offbeat jobs in the first place?

RESEARCH TOPICS, see page 188.

UNIT 2

Building a Better Community

①FOCUS ON THE TOPIC

A PREDICT

Look at the pictures and discuss the questions with the class.

1. Which picture shows a city, a suburb, or a small town? How do you know?

2. Read the title of the unit. What kind of communities do you think the unit will be about?

17

Work in a small group. Discuss the questions. Use the words in the box to help you.

apartments	friendly	safe
buses and trains	houses	shopping malls
businesses	nature	stores
clean	neighborhoods	tall buildings
crowded	noisy	traffic
dangerous	quiet	trees
freeways	rural	urban (in cities and suburbs)

1. How is the city different from the suburbs, small towns, and the country?

   The city is _____.   The city has _____.

   The suburbs are _____.   The suburbs have _____.

   Small towns are _____.   Small towns have _____.

2. Read the graph. How did the world population in cities change between 1955 and 2005? Where was the biggest change? Where was the smallest change?

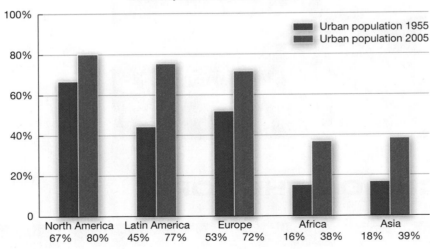

World Population in Cities—1955 and 2005

Urban population 1955
Urban population 2005

	North America	Latin America	Europe	Africa	Asia
1955	67%	45%	53%	16%	18%
2005	80%	77%	72%	38%	39%

3. What kind of community do you live in: a city, a suburb, or a small town? What do you like about your community? What don't you like?

1 CD 1 ⑬ *Read and listen to a radio news report.*

HOST: Good afternoon and welcome to *Newsline*. This is Joanne Williams. Tonight we begin our series on communities. First, we'll talk about **(1) urban** communities. About 50 percent of people in the world live in urban areas, in cities and suburbs. In North America about 80 percent of people live in urban areas, mostly in suburbs . . . and, like it or not, **(2) typical** American suburbs are **(3) designed** to be **(4) convenient** for driving. Homes, businesses, and shopping centers are usually far away from each other. So, most people have to drive to get from one place to another, instead of walking or taking **(5) public transportation**. Some people rent apartments or buy **(6) condominiums**, but most people still want the American dream—to own their own home with a backyard, a driveway, and a garage. However, more people are starting to complain that typical suburbs are bad for the **(7) environment** because they are growing and taking away nature and green spaces. And all of those people driving cars can create too much traffic. Others say that people in suburbs are **(8) isolated** from each other, so they don't get to know each other or build a **(9) sense of community**. What do you think? In this evening's program, we're going to talk about a new type of urban design that wants to change all of this. It's called New Urbanism.

2 *Write the number of each boldfaced word from the paragraph next to its definition.*

___5___ **a.** buses and trains that run at regular times and that anyone can use

_____ **b.** not connected; separate

_____ **c.** caring and friendly feeling that people in a particular area share

_____ **d.** useful because it saves time or doesn't cause problems; close or easy to get to

_____ **e.** apartments that people own

_____ **f.** relating to cities

_____ **g.** usual

_____ **h.** the air, water, and land where plants, animals, and people live

_____ **i.** planned or developed by someone for a reason

A LISTENING ONE: A New-Urbanist Community

CD1
14
Listen to the beginning of a radio news report about a new community. Read each question and circle the correct answer.

1. Where is Roy Martinez?

   a. at the radio station
   b. in a new suburb called Kentville
   c. at Elizabeth Jones's house

2. What do you think Roy will learn about the community? (*Circle more than one answer.*)

   a. where it is
   b. who lives there
   c. what it looks like
   d. how much it costs to live there
   e. how it is different from a typical suburb

◖ LISTEN FOR MAIN IDEAS

CD1
15
Read the list of ways that new-urbanist communities are designed to be different from typical suburbs. Listen to the complete radio interview. Check (✓) the things that are true about Kentville.

New-urbanist communities . . .

_____ 1. are convenient for walking.

_____ 2. are connected to public transportation.

_____ 3. are places where people have a sense of community.

_____ 4. have many parks and trees.

_____ 5. have different kinds of housing near each other.

A new-urbanist community

◖ LISTEN FOR DETAILS

CD 1 *Listen to the complete radio interview again. Then read each statement. Write*
16 ***T** (true) or **F** (false).*

_____ **1.** In Kentville, the housing and businesses are far from each other.

_____ **2.** Kentville is not a friendly place.

_____ **3.** People in Kentville want to walk more.

_____ **4.** The sidewalks are wide.

_____ **5.** There are special parking lots for cars.

_____ **6.** The garages are in front of the houses.

_____ **7.** The houses are built close together.

_____ **8.** The houses are close to the street and have front porches.

_____ **9.** Elizabeth Jones thinks people will stay in their houses or in their backyards.

_____ **10.** Elizabeth Jones wanted to build a community where different kinds of people would live together and get to know each other.

Now go back to Section 2A (question 2) on page 20. Were your predictions correct?

◖ MAKE INFERENCES

Listen to three excerpts from the interview. Then decide whether the person would agree or disagree with the statement. Circle your answer.

CD 1
17 **Excerpt One**

   1. "There's nothing wrong with people driving a lot."
      Would Roy agree or disagree?

      a. agree   **b.** disagree

   2. "Cars are convenient."
      Would Elizabeth agree or disagree?

      a. agree   **b.** disagree

CD 1
18 **Excerpt Two**

   1. "It's surprising that people want to walk more."
      Would Roy agree or disagree?

      a. agree   **b.** disagree

   2. "People don't like to walk."
      Would Elizabeth agree or disagree?

      a. agree   **b.** disagree

(continued on next page)

CD 7
19 Excerpt Three

1. "Different kinds of people live near each other in typical suburbs."
   Would Elizabeth agree or disagree?

   a. agree   **b.** disagree

2. "Most people want to be around people that are different."
   Would Roy agree or disagree?

   a. agree   **b.** disagree

Compare your answers with a classmate's. Explain your answers using details from the listening.

◀ EXPRESS OPINIONS

Work in a small group. Discuss your opinions using the sentence starters.

1. I would / wouldn't like to live in Kentville because . . .

2. I prefer to live around people who are similar to / different from me because . . .

3. I usually get around my town / city by . . .

B LISTENING TWO: Let's Hear from Our Listeners

CD 7
20 *In Listening Two, the radio show host is taking calls from the listening audience. The callers are discussing their opinions about Kentville. Listen and circle the best answer to complete each statement.*

1. The first caller _____.
   a. doesn't live in Kentville
   b. doesn't like living in Kentville
   c. thinks Kentville is a great place to live

2. The first caller thinks there isn't enough public transportation _____.
   a. in Kentville
   b. between Kentville and other places
   c. in other suburbs

3. The second caller grew up _____.
   a. in a city
   b. in a suburb
   c. in a small town

4. The second caller thinks a sense of community _____.
   a. is not important
   b. is easy to create in Kentville
   c. takes time to build

5. The third caller lives _____.
   a. in a city
   b. in Kentville
   c. in a suburb

6. The third caller thinks Kentville is _____.
   a. crowded
   b. boring
   c. exciting

C INTEGRATE LISTENINGS ONE AND TWO

◀ STEP 1: Organize

Work with a partner. In the chart, write the positive things and negative things about Kentville that each person mentions. If there isn't enough information, leave the space blank.

	POSITIVE	NEGATIVE
Elizabeth Jones	It's convenient for walking.	
Caller One		
Caller Two		
Caller Three		

◀ STEP 2: Synthesize

Work with the same partner. Debate the topic: "Is Kentville a good place to live?" One partner argues that Kentville is a good place to live and the other partner argues that it isn't. Use the information from Step 1 to support your opinion. Then switch partners and roles.

Examples

I think Kentville is a good place to live because it's convenient for walking.

I disagree. I don't think Kentville is a good place to live because ...

A VOCABULARY

◖ REVIEW

Complete the conversation with the words from the box. Then practice reading the conversation aloud with a partner.

boring	environment	sense of community
convenient	exciting	stuck in traffic
crazy about	isolated	
~~crowded~~	public transportation	

A: Hi there! So, how do you like it here in Mumbai?

B: Well, I like it all right, but there are so many people everywhere!

A: Yeah, it sure is _____crowded_____.
　　　　　　　　　　　　　　1.

B: And the streets are so busy—with cars, buses, motorcycles, bicycles . . . I spend a

　　lot of time _____ on my way to school.
　　　　　　　　　　　　2.

A: So how do you get to school?

B: I take the bus. It's good that the city has so much _____. But
　　　　　　　　　　　　　　　　　　　　　　　　　　　　3.

　　those buses are so bad for the _____!
　　　　　　　　　　　　　　　　　　4.

A: So it sounds like you aren't so _____ living here.
　　　　　　　　　　　　　　　　　　5.

B: Well, it's not so bad. There's so much to see and do here compared to my hometown. It really is a(n) _____ place to live. And it's good
6.
that my apartment is in a _____ location. There are
7.
markets, shops, restaurants, and even a movie theater near my house.

A: So, do you ever get homesick?

B: Oh sure. I really miss my family and my hometown. It's so beautiful and peaceful there, but it's really far away from everything.

A: So, your hometown is pretty _____?
8.

B: Yeah, and there really isn't much to do there. You'd probably think it's

_____. But what I like is that I know everyone and everyone
9.

knows me. I really feel connected. There's a real _____.
10.

A: Do you think you'll ever go back?

B: Well, I'll probably have to stay in the city to find a job. But I hope I can move back someday.

◖ **EXPAND**

1 *Read the e-mail. Then locate the places described in the e-mail on the map on page 27.*

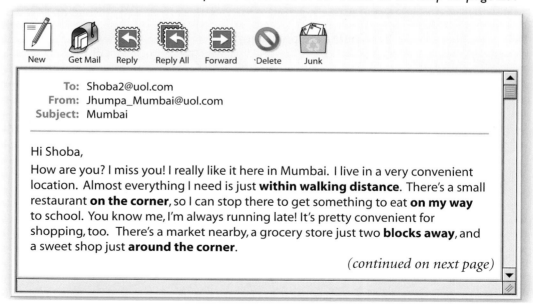

To: Shoba2@uol.com
From: Jhumpa_Mumbai@uol.com
Subject: Mumbai

Hi Shoba,
How are you? I miss you! I really like it here in Mumbai. I live in a very convenient location. Almost everything I need is just **within walking distance**. There's a small restaurant **on the corner**, so I can stop there to get something to eat **on my way** to school. You know me, I'm always running late! It's pretty convenient for shopping, too. There's a market nearby, a grocery store just two **blocks away**, and a sweet shop just **around the corner**.

(continued on next page)

Best of all, there's a small park nearby. On nice days, I like to sit outside and read a book, or watch the people walking by. And there are so many movie theaters here! There's one just **down the street** from my apartment, and I go there every chance I get. The only problem is my college is a little **out of the way** so I usually take a bus to get there. Luckily there's a bus stop **across the street** from my apartment.

I hope you'll come visit me. You're welcome anytime. I'm **on** Main Road **between** Bazaar Road and Das Street. Maybe you can come next weekend!

See you soon,

Jhumpa

2 Work with a partner. Student A, ask the questions about the places in Jhumpa's neighborhood. Student B, look at the map on page 27 and use the words from the box to complete your answers. Switch roles after item 5.

across the street	down	on the way
around the corner	next door	out of the way
between	on	within walking distance
blocks away	on the corner	

Student A

1. Where's the clothing store?

2. Where's the pharmacy?

3. You're at Jhumpa's apartment. Where's the movie theater?

4. You're at the clinic. Where's the bookstore?

5. You're at the shoe store. Where's the clothing store?

Student B

It's _____ of Main Road and Cadel Road.

It's _____ from the clinic.

It's _____ the street.

It's _____ from the clinic.

It's _____.

6. You're at the train station. Where's the park?

It's three _____.

7. You're at the post office and going to the market. Where's the college?

It's _____.

8. You're at the grocery store and going to Jhumpa's apartment. Where's the sweet shop?

It's _____ to Jhumpa's apartment.

9. You're at the college. Where's the train station?

It isn't _____ _____.

10. Where's the shoe store?

It's _____ Main Road. It's _____ Das Street and Cadel Road.

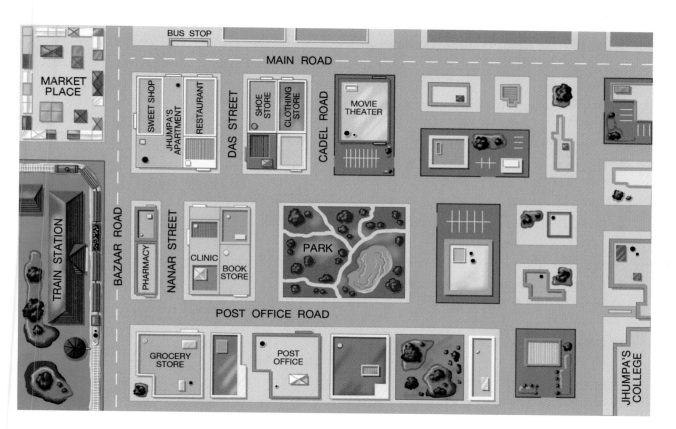

◖ CREATE

Work with a partner. Interview each other about where you live. Write your partner's answers in the chart. Use the boldfaced words and vocabulary from Review and Expand to answer the questions. When you finish, share your partner's information with the class.

QUESTIONS	PARTNER'S ANSWERS
1. What street do you live **on**?	
2. Do you live in a **convenient** location, or is it **out of the way**?	
3. Do you take **public transportation** to get to school? What type?	
4. Do you ever get **stuck in traffic**? If so, where?	
5. Do you stop anywhere **on the way** to school? Where do you stop?	
6. Do you know your neighbors **next** door?	
7. Do you feel **a sense of community** where you live, or do you feel **isolated**?	
8. Do you think your community is **exciting** or **boring**?	
9. Name something in your community that you aren't **crazy about**.	

1 *Read the sentences. Look at the underlined words. Then answer the questions.*

<u>This</u> city is clean. <u>That one</u> is polluted.

<u>These</u> apartments are in a convenient location. <u>Those</u> are out of the way.

a. Is the word *city* singular or plural? What word comes before it?

b. What word comes after *that*? What does it refer to?

c. Is the word *apartments* singular or plural? What word comes before it?

d. What does the word *those* refer to?

THIS / THAT / THESE / THOSE AND ONE	
1. Use **this**, **that**, **these**, and **those** to identify persons or things.	Cities are big. **This** city is the biggest.
2. Use **this** or **that** to talk about a singular noun. **This** refers to a person or thing near you. **That** refers to a person or thing far from you.	**This** is my house. **That's** my friend's house.
3. Use **these** or **those** to talk about plural nouns. **These** refers to people or things near you. **Those** refers to people or things far away.	**These** condominiums are big. **Those** condominiums are small.
4. **This**, **that**, **these**, and **those** can be pronouns or adjectives.	**This** is my car. **This** car is blue.
5. Use **one** after **this** or **that**. Do not use **ones** after **these** or **those**.	**A:** Do you live in **this** apartment? **B:** No, I don't live in **this one**. I live in **that one**. **A:** Do you shop at **these** stores? **B:** No, I don't shop at **these**. I shop at **those**.

2 *Work with a partner. Look at the maps and take turns comparing the typical suburb and the New-urbanist suburb. Make as many statements as you can about the places on the maps.*

Examples

That school in the typical suburb map is not within walking distance to the houses.

Those houses are very close together.

Typical Suburb

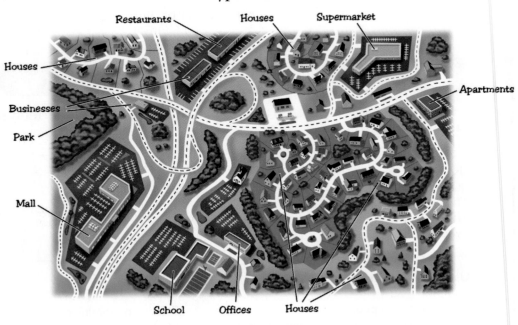

New-Urbanist Suburb

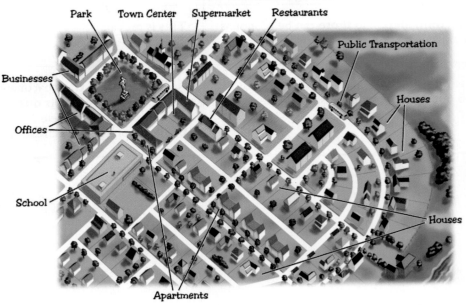

◀ PRONUNCIATION: TH Sounds

Look at the picture of how you say the TH sounds in English:

The tip of the tongue is between your teeth. When you say the first sound in *this* (/ð/), your vocal cords vibrate. When you say the first sound in *thing* (/θ/), your vocal cords don't vibrate.

tongue

CD 1
21 *Listen to the boldfaced sounds in this sentence.*

Every**th**ing in **th**is town is wi**th**in walking distance.

1 **CD 1** *Listen to the words and phrases and repeat them.*
22 *Then practice saying the words with a partner.*

1. theater
2. these
3. this evening
4. then
5. path

6. nothing
7. something
8. everything
9. either
10. clothing store

2 **CD 1** *Listen to the conversation. Write the words in the blanks. All of the missing words*
23 *have TH sounds. Check your answers with the class. Then practice the conversation*
with a partner. Pronounce words with TH carefully.

1. **A:** How far away is the _____? Should we drive?

2. **B:** No, _____'s _____ walking distance in

   _____ town. Mom and Dad don't have to drive anywhere.

3. **A:** _____'s great. I don't like driving, _____. But,

   you know, the houses are really close _____. How do

   _____ feel about _____?

4. **B:** _____ like it. You know, _____'s

   _____ wrong _____ being close to your

   neighbors.

3 Work with a partner. People have different opinions about the best place to live. Make short conversations with your partner about the living situations listed in the box. Use the example conversation as a model. Give reasons for your answers. Try to pronounce TH correctly.

> living in a big city
>
> living in a small town
>
> living in a town like Kentville
>
> living in a typical suburb

Example

STUDENT A: What do you think about ___living in a big city___ ?

STUDENT B: There's nothing wrong with ___living in a big city. It's exciting. There___ ___are a lot of things to do.___

OR

I think there's something wrong with ___living in a big city. You never___ ___get to know your neighbors. Life is too fast.___

◖FUNCTION: Expressing Agreement

EXPRESSING AGREEMENT	
1. In conversation, when we want to agree with an affirmative statement someone has just made, we can use the word **too** in our response.	**A:** I live in the suburbs. **B:** I live in the suburbs, **too**. OR I do, **too**. **A:** My house is small. **B:** My house is small, **too**. OR My house is, **too**.
2. When we want to agree with a negative statement someone has just made, we can use **not . . . either** in our response.	**A:** I don't like the city. **B:** I don't like the city **either**. OR I don't **either**.

1 *Work with a partner. Read the conversations. Circle the correct word to complete each response and write the short form on the line. Then practice reading the conversations aloud. Switch roles with each conversation.*

Example

A: My house doesn't have a front yard.
B: My house doesn't have a front yard <u>too / (either)</u>.

    <u>My house doesn't either.</u>

  1. **A:** I like to use public transportation.

     B: I like to use public transportation <u>too / either</u>.

     _____

  2. **A:** I don't live in a condominium.

     B: I don't live in a condominium <u>too / either</u>.

     _____

  3. **A:** My neighborhood is crowded.

     B: My neighborhood is crowded <u>too / either</u>.

     _____

  4. **A:** I don't live near a market.

     B: I don't live near a market <u>too / either</u>.

     _____

  5. **A:** The houses in my neighborhood are old.

     B: The houses in my neighborhood are old <u>too / either</u>.

     _____

2 *Work with a partner. Take turns reading the statements and responding with statements about your town or city.*

Example

A: Dublin isn't very polluted.
B: My city isn't either.
       OR
B: My city is very polluted.

  1. Most people in Hong Kong live in apartments.

  2. Zurich doesn't have a lot of tall buildings.

(continued on next page)

3. Most people in New York City don't have a car.

4. Los Angeles doesn't have a subway system.

5. Most people in Sydney drive to work.

6. Toronto has a lot of parks.

◖ PRODUCTION: Redesigning a Neighborhood

Imagine you are urban designers. **Your job is to redesign an area in your community**. It could be the neighborhood around your school or another neighborhood you all know. Try to use the vocabulary, grammar, pronunciation, and language for expressing agreement that you learned in the unit.*

Work in a small group. Follow the steps.

Step 1: Choose a neighborhood in your own community to re-design. Draw a map that shows several blocks of the neighborhood on a piece of paper. Label the streets, housing, schools, businesses, and public transportation stops on the map.

Step 2: Decide what things you want to keep and what you want to change. Each person in the group should suggest something to keep and something to change, and say why.

Example

A: I want to keep this coffee shop next to the school because it's convenient.
B: I do, too. But I think these houses are too isolated. I want to put a train stop on this corner, so these people can take the train to work.

Step 3: Draw a picture of your newly designed neighborhood.

Step 4: Present your original map and your new community map to the class. Show the class the changes you made and explain why you made them.

Listening Activity

After you listen to your classmates, choose the community you like best. Explain why you like that community.

---

*For Alternative Speaking Topics, see page 35.

ALTERNATIVE SPEAKING TOPICS

Work in a small group. Discuss the questions.

1. As urban areas get bigger and spread out, more land in the country is developed. Do you think that urban designers should try to save nature and green spaces? If so, how should they do it? Or do you think people should continue to develop this land if they want to? Why do you think so?

2. Do you prefer to live close to your neighbors, or do you prefer to have more space? Why?

3. Do you think the government should spend more money on public transportation or more money on roads for cars? Why?

RESEARCH TOPICS, see page 188.

A Penny Saved Is a Penny Earned

①FOCUS ON THE TOPIC

A PREDICT

Look at the picture and discuss the questions with the class.

1. What is the man's problem?

2. What do you think he should do?

3. Read the title of the unit. It is a famous American saying. What do you think it means?

SHARE INFORMATION

1 *How do you usually pay for the things you need? Write* **often**, **sometimes**, *or* **never**.

_____ **cash**

_____ **checks**

_____ **credit cards** (plastic cards you use to buy things and pay later)

_____ **loans** (money you borrow and pay back later)

2 *Work in a small group. Answer the questions.*

1. In your group, what is the most common way to pay for things? What is the least common way?

2. What do you think is the best way to pay for things when you want to save money? Why do you think so?

C **BACKGROUND** AND **VOCABULARY**

1 CD1 24 *Read and listen to the timeline and the newspaper article about the history of money and bartering.*

MONEY SERIES

PART ONE: THE HISTORY OF MONEY AND BARTERING

9000 B.C.E.[1]	640 B.C.E.	806 C.E.[2]	1160	1619
farm animals and plants used as money	first metal coins	first paper money made in China	first bank loans made in England	tobacco used as money in Virginia

1659	1950	1984	1995
first check used in England	first credit card	first ATM machines	first electronic cash cards

[1] **B.C.E.** = Before the Common Era
[2] **C.E.** = the Common Era

efore people used money, they used other things that were **valuable** to them, such as plants or animals, to pay for things. Over the years, people developed more convenient ways to buy things such as loans, checks, and credit cards. Another convenient type of money is electronic money. Electronic money **represents** real money but can be saved on a computer or on an electronic cash card. Electronic money makes it easy to send money over the Internet. Today, there are many ways to buy things. But it is also easy to **spend** too much money. People can have problems when they spend more than they **earn**. As a result, many people are often looking for ways to save money.

One way for people to save money is bartering. Bartering means **trading** one thing for another without using money. For example, one person might **exchange** some food for some clothing or other item with **equal** value.

Before people used money, they bartered for the things they needed. Today, people, businesses, and governments still barter as a way to save money. For example, a business might barter for goods, such as machines, or **services** that another business can do for them. Some people use the Internet to find other people interested in bartering. Other people use community barter **networks**. A barter network is a group of people that trade with each other. A barter network **provides** its **members** with the chance to save money and get to know other people in their community.

2 *Choose the best definition for each word. Circle your answers.*

1. **valuable**   (a.) useful, important   **b.** living
2. **represents**   **a.** pays for something   (b.) is a sign for something
3. **spend**   (a.) pay money   **b.** get money
4. **earn**   (a.) get money by working   **b.** pay money
5. **trading**   (a.) giving one thing for another   **b.** not spending money
6. **exchange**   **a.** buy a new thing   (b.) give one thing for another
7. **equal**   (a.) different   (b) the same
8. **service**   (a.) something you do for someone   **b.** a thing you buy someone
9. **network**   (a) group of people with the same interests   **b.** people in a community
10. **provides**   (a) gives   (b.) gets
11. **member**   (a) person who belongs to a group   **b.** person who barters

② FOCUS ON LISTENING

Ⓐ LISTENING ONE: A Barter Network

1 CD 1 ㉕ *Listen to the beginning of* **A Bartner Network.** *Then read each question and circle the correct answer.*

    1. What are you listening to?
        a. a radio announcement
        b. a meeting
        c. a class

    2. Who is listening while Carol speaks?
        a. members of the barter network
        b. people who work for the barter network
        c. people who are interested in joining the network

2 *Make predictions. Circle more than one answer.*

    1. Carol is going to discuss . . .
        a. what bartering is.
        b. why people like to barter.
        c. how to use the barter network.
        d. how to join the network.

    2. Carol is going to give this information:
        a. examples of things people barter
        b. how old the barter network is
        c. how many members belong to the network
        d. names of other members
        e. how to find other members
        f. an example of a barter exchange

◖ LISTEN FOR MAIN IDEAS

CD 1 ㉖ *Listen to the whole discussion about the City Barter Network. Put a check (✓) next to the things that members do.*

Members . . .

_____ barter for things and services.   _____ earn Time Dollars.

_____ only barter for services.   _____ use Time Dollars to buy services.

_____ need to provide a service before   _____ spend money.
       they can get one.

_____ earn money.

◖ LISTEN FOR DETAILS

^{C D 7}
27 *Listen to the barter network meeting again. Then read each statement. Write* **T** *(true) or* **F** *(false).*

_____ 1. Members can list their services on a website.

_____ 2. Most members provide services like cooking, cleaning, or fixing things.

_____ 3. Members don't provide unusual services like taking photographs or giving music lessons.

_____ 4. Some services are more valuable than others.

_____ 5. Carol spent two hours cleaning another member's house.

_____ 6. A member spent one hour fixing Carol's computer.

_____ 7. The man doesn't think he has skills.

_____ 8. Carol needs someone to walk her dog.

Now go back to Section 2A, Exercise 2 on page 40. Were your predictions correct?

◖ MAKE INFERENCES

Listen to three excerpts from the barter network meeting. After listening to each excerpt, read the questions and circle the correct answers.

^{C D 7}
28 **Excerpt One**

1. How does the man feel about exchanging services?
   a. He feels excited.
   b. He doesn't feel excited.

2. How do you know?
   a. His voice is flat.
   b. His voice rises and falls.

^{C D 7}
29 **Excerpt Two**

1. How does the woman feel about getting piano lessons?
   a. She feels excited.
   b. She doesn't feel excited.

2. How do you know?
   a. Her voice is flat.
   b. Her voice rises and falls.

(continued on next page)

A Penny Saved Is a Penny Earned **41**

CD 7
30 **Excerpt Three**

1. How does the man feel about the woman's question?

   a. He's surprised.
   b. He isn't surprised.

2. How do you know?

   a. His voice is flat.
   b. His voice rises.

◀ EXPRESS OPINIONS

Read the statements and circle agree or disagree. Then discuss your answers with the class.

1. I'd like to join a barter network.	agree	disagree
2. Bartering is a good way for me to save money.	agree	disagree
3. I like to save money by buying used things.	agree	disagree
4. Buying new things helps me feel good.	agree	disagree

B LISTENING TWO: The Compact

CD 7
31 *Listen to the conversation between two members of the City Barter Network. Circle the best answer to complete each statement.*

Used items in a thrift store

1. The Compact is a group of people who promised _____.

   a. to barter for a year
   b. not to buy anything new for a year

2. Members of the Compact can buy new _____.

   a. food, medicine, and necessities
   b. food, cars, and necessities

3. The members of the Compact think _____.

   a. clothes, cars, and electronics are too expensive
   b. most people have too much stuff they don't need

4. Members of the Compact _____ to get what they need.

    a. borrow, buy things used, or barter

    b. buy used things and barter for food

5. Mark needed to buy _____.

    a. new paint

    b. a new house

6. There are _____ of members in the Compact.

    a. hundreds

    b. thousands

7. Natalie likes shopping for _____.

    a. used clothes

    b. new clothes

C INTEGRATE LISTENINGS ONE AND TWO

◖ STEP 1: Organize

1 *Look at the list of goods (things you can buy) and services (things you pay people to do for you) mentioned in the listenings. Write each item in the correct column in the chart.*

car	fix a television	medicine
~~clean someone's house~~	food	paint someone's house
clothes	give someone piano lessons	walk someone's dog
computer		

GOODS	SERVICES
	clean someone's house

2 *How can members of the Compact get the goods and services they need? Write each good and service from the chart in the correct place on the graphic organizer. Then compare your answers with a classmate's.*

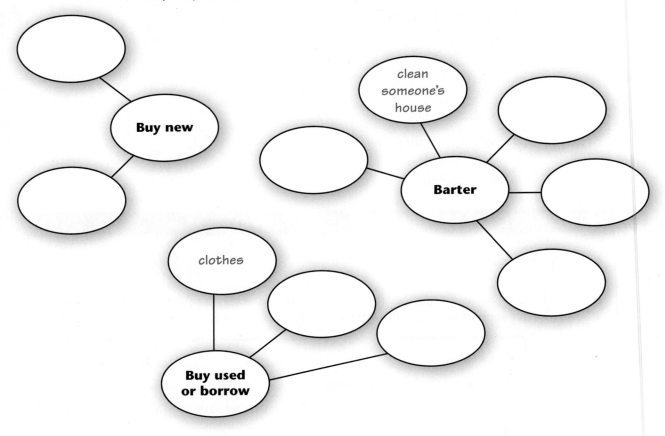

◖ **STEP 2: Synthesize**

Work with a partner. Imagine you are in the City Barter Network and the Compact. Student A, say what you need. Student B, suggest a way to get each thing. Use the information from Step 1.

Example

A: I want someone to clean my house.
B: You can get that by bartering.

3 FOCUS ON SPEAKING

A VOCABULARY

REVIEW

Complete the conversations with words from the box. Use the underlined words to help you. Then work with a partner. Practice reading the conversations aloud. Switch roles after item 4.

borrow	exchange	services	stuff	valuable
equal	necessity	spend	~~used~~	

1. **A:** I bought a chair at a thrift store yesterday. <u>It isn't new,</u> but it's very nice.

   B: Do you really like to buy _____used_____ things?

2. **A:** This sweater is too big. I need to take it back to the store and <u>trade it</u> for a smaller one.

   B: Does that store let you _____exchange_____ things?

3. **A:** Do you want to go shopping? I need to get some <u>things</u> for my apartment.

   B: No, thanks. I already have too much _____stuff_____.

4. **A:** I wish I knew how to do something <u>useful</u>, like fixing cars.

   B: Yeah, you're right. Fixing cars is a _____valuable_____ skill.

5. **A:** I <u>need</u> to buy a new television.

   B: Really? Is a television really a _____necessity_____?

6. **A:** I don't want to <u>pay</u> a lot of money for a television.

   B: How much do you want to _____spend_____?

7. **A:** That department store <u>does so many things</u> for you. They even have personal shoppers, people who help you choose what to buy.

   B: Yeah, they do offer a lot of _____services_____.

8. **A:** Do you think these two cameras are <u>the same</u>?

   B: Yeah, I think they are pretty _____equal_____.

9. **A:** My car broke down. Can I <u>use yours</u> to get to school today?

   B: Sure, you can _____borrow_____ it anytime.

A Penny Saved Is a Penny Earned   **45**

1 *Read the newsletter article about flea markets.*

The Barter Network Newsletter
By Carol Meyer

This Week's Money-Saving Tip: Flea Markets

Are you looking for another way to save money? If so, you should try shopping at flea markets. Flea markets are a great place to find lots of interesting used items without **paying an arm and a leg**. There are wonderful flea markets all over the world, including Maxwell's Street Market in Chicago, the Grand Bazaar in Istanbul, La Merced in Mexico City, or the Marche aux Puces in Paris.

Did you know that our city has a flea market too? It meets every Saturday in the parking lot of South High School. People come to buy and sell all kinds of things: furniture, clothes, artwork, electronics, and more. Some of the items are expensive. For example, you may not be able **to afford** some of the antiques. But most of the items are really cheap. You can really find some great **bargains**. The best way to save money is **to bargain** with the sellers. That's how I **got a good deal** on a jacket last Saturday. At first, the seller asked $100 for it, but I bargained with him until he agreed to take only $50. My friend got an even better deal. She bought a painting that only **cost** $10. Later, she found out that the painting is **worth** $300! So, if you are looking for a fun new way to save money, you should head to the flea market. It's really **worth it**.

2 *Match the words and phrases on the left with the definitions on the right.*

_____ 1. to pay an arm and a leg

_____ 2. to afford

_____ 3. a bargain

_____ 4. to bargain

_____ 5. to get a good deal

_____ 6. to cost

_____ 7. to be worth

_____ 8. to be worth it

a. to have a particular value

b. to have a particular price

c. to have enough money to pay for something

d. to get a good price on something

e. to spend a lot of money

f. to discuss the price of something you are buying

g. to be good to do even though you made an effort

h. something you buy for less than the usual price

Work in a small group. Take turns asking and answering the questions. Use the boldfaced words and vocabulary from Review and Expand in your answers.

1. Do you like **to bargain** with sellers when you shop? Do you bargain when you buy from street vendors? Why or why not?

2. Do you like to buy things **used**? Why or why not? If yes, what are some things that you like to buy used? What are some things you never buy used?

3. Name a store or place to shop that you think has good **bargains**. What kinds of bargains can you get there?

4. Name something you bought that you **got a good deal** on. Where did you get it? Why do you think it was a good deal?

5. Do you have a lot of **stuff** in your house? What do you usually do with stuff that you don't use anymore—do you prefer to keep it, throw it away, or give it to someone else?

6. Name something you own that was **cheap** to buy. How much did it cost? Name something that you **paid an arm and a leg** for.

7. Do you own something that is **worth** more now than when you bought it? How much did you **spend** on it? What is it worth now?

B GRAMMAR: Comparative Adjectives

1 *Read the sentences. Look at the underlined words. Then answer the questions.*

I need to find a <u>cheaper</u> place to shop.

The department store is <u>bigger</u> than the thrift store.

a. What is the adjective in the first sentence? What does it describe? What two letters does the adjective end with?

b. What is the adjective in the second sentence? What does it describe? What word comes after *bigger*?

COMPARATIVE ADJECTIVES

1. Use the comparative form of the adjective to compare two people, places, or things. Use **than** before the second person, place, or thing.	This car is **cheaper *than*** that one.
2. Add **–er** to form the comparative of short (one-syllable) adjectives. Add **–r** if the adjective ends in **e**.	cheap cheap**er** old old**er** close close**r**
3. When a one-syllable adjective ends in a consonant + vowel + consonant, double the last consonant and add **–er**.	big big**ger** hot hot**ter**
4. When two-syllable adjectives end in **–y**, change the **y** to **i** and add **–er**.	easy eas**ier** funny funn**ier**
5. Some adjectives have irregular comparative forms.	good **better** bad **worse**
6. To form the comparative of most adjectives of two or more syllables, add **more** before the adjective. **Less** is the opposite of **more**.	No service is **more valuable** than another one. Used clothing is **less expensive** than new clothing.

2 *Work with a partner. Look at the ads for the cars. Take turns making sentences comparing the two cars. Use the adjectives from the box. Then say which car you would like to buy and why.*

bad for the environment	easy to park	nice
big	expensive	old
cheap to drive	good for a big family	safe
comfortable		

Example

A: The Indulge is bigger than the Pee Wee.
B: The Indulge is more expensive than the Pee Wee.

Introducing the new

INDULGE

Buy a new
Indulge
**and drive in comfort,
style, and safety for only $50,000!**

This week's special: a used

Pee Wee

This Pee Wee
is almost new, and it
runs great! It gets excellent
gas mileage, and it's on sale now for only $4,000!

3 *Work with a partner. Write eight sentences comparing the Indulge and the Pee Wee.
Read them aloud to the class.*

C SPEAKING

◀ PRONUNCIATION: Numbers and Prices

When we say the numbers 13 through 19, *-teen* is stressed and the letter *t* in *-teen*
sounds like /t/. When we say the numbers 20, 30, 40, 50, 60, 70, 80, and 90, the first
syllable is stressed and the letter *t* in *-ty* sounds like a "fast" /d/.

CD 1
32 *Listen to the examples.*

13	16	19
/thirtéen/	/sixtéen/	/ninetéen/

30	60	90
/thírdy/	/síxdy/	/nínedy/

There are two ways to say prices.

CD 1
32 *Listen to the examples.*

$4.29 four dollars and twenty-nine cents

 four twenty-nine

$53.99 fifty-three dollars and ninety-nine cents

 fifty-three ninety-nine

1 *Listen to the numbers. Circle the number you hear.*

    1. 13   30

    2. 14   40

    3. 15   50

    4. 16   60

    5. 17   70

    6. 18   80

    7. 19   90

2 *Work with a partner. Look at the numbers in Exercise 1. Take turns. Say a number. Remember to stress the correct syllable. Your partner points to the number you say.*

3 CD 1 34 *Listen and write the prices you hear. Then practice saying them aloud in two different ways.*

    1. $ _____

    2. $ _____

    3. $ _____

    4. $ _____

    5. $ _____

4 *Work with a partner. Take turns asking each other how much you usually spend on the items listed. Write your partner's answers. Share the information with your classmates.*

Example

A: How much do you usually spend on a haircut?
B: I spend thirty dollars. How about you?
A: I spend fifteen dollars.

    1. a haircut $ _____

    2. a movie ticket $ _____

    3. your phone bill $ _____

    4. a meal in a restaurant $ _____

◀ FUNCTION: Negotiating—Making Suggestions and Coming to an Agreement

When two or more people need to make a decision together, they need to negotiate; they need to come to an agreement. When negotiating, you need to make suggestions until each person agrees.

MAKING SUGGESTIONS	AGREEING WITH SUGGESTIONS	DISAGREEING WITH SUGGESTIONS
Let's buy this chair. **Why don't** we go to the thrift store? **How about** buying a used car instead of a new one? **Would you** like to sell your computer?	OK. / All right. That's fine with me. That's a good idea. Let's do it. It's a deal. OK. Why not?	Well, I don't know. How about …? I have another idea. Why don't we …? I don't think so.

1 *Look at the list of things. Pretend you have $2,500 to buy things for your new house or apartment. Make a list of the things you would like to get.*

used couch—$100

new couch—$650

large armchair—$300

large floor rug—$200

lamp—$25

bookcase—$115

painting—$175

video-game player—$200

plants—$50

pet kitten—$75

pet dog—$130

computer—$800

CD player—$250

used piano—$300

small used television—$85

large new television—$700

Your List

_____   _____   _____

_____   _____   _____

2 *Now work in a small group. Take turns suggesting things to buy. When everyone agrees, write your group's list below.*

Example

A: Let's buy the used couch for $100.
B: Well, I don't know. I don't want a used couch. How about buying the new one?
C: But it costs a lot. Why don't we buy the chair?

Your Group's List

_____   _____   _____

_____   _____   _____

3 *Share your group's list with another group. Explain why your group chose each thing. The other group listens and answers. Did you choose the same things? Why or why not?*

◖ **PRODUCTION: Bartering**

> In this activity, you will ***practice bartering for goods and services with your classmates***. Try to use the vocabulary, grammar, pronunciation, and language for negotiating that you learned in the unit.*

Follow the steps.

Step 1: Get five blank cards. On four of the cards write the following:

   a. name of an item you would like to exchange (and a drawing, if you'd like)

   b. how old it is

   c. how much money you think it is worth now.

Do this for four items. On the fifth card, write a service you can provide, such as cook dinner.

Step 2: Go around the class and barter with your classmates. Compare your items and services and negotiate with each other until you come to an agreement. When you come to an agreement, trade your cards.

_____
*For Alternative Speaking Topics, see page 53.

Example

A: How about trading your television for my computer?
B: But my television is newer than your computer.
A: Yeah, but my computer is more valuable.
B: Thanks, but that's not worth it. I want to keep looking.
OR
B: OK. It's a deal.

Step 3: Report your exchanges to the class.

Example

A: I traded a two-year-old television worth $300 for a three-year-old computer worth $350.
B: That's a pretty good deal.
C: Well, I paid an arm and a leg for a TV.

Listening Activity

Listen to your classmates' reports. Who made the most exchanges? Who got the best deal?

ALTERNATIVE SPEAKING TOPICS

Work in a small group. Discuss the questions.

1. Do you think that most people have too much stuff? Why or why not? Give examples.

2. Do you think the Compact is a good idea or a bad idea? Why? Could you keep a promise not to buy anything new for a year? Explain.

RESEARCH TOPICS, see page 189.

4 Innocent or Guilty?

1 FOCUS ON THE TOPIC

A PREDICT

Look at the picture and discuss the questions with the class.

1. Where are the people?

2. Why do you think the man is there?

3. What do you think the man and woman are talking about?

1 *Police get a lot of information about criminals from people on the street who saw what happened. However, often these people do not remember the details. How well can you remember details? Work with a partner. Complete the activity.*

Student A, look at the photograph of the person on page 181. Study it for <u>two</u> minutes and close your book. Then describe what you saw to Student B. Use as many details as possible.

Student B, after Student A finishes describing the photo, draw a picture or use words to describe the person. Use the box below. Switch roles.

Student B, look at the photograph of the person on page 182 for <u>two</u> minutes and close your book. Describe the photograph to Student A. Use as many details as possible. Student A, draw or describe the picture.

2 *Look at the two photographs on pages 181 and 182. Answer the questions.*

1. Do the drawings or descriptions match the photos? How are they different?

2. Do you think it is easy to remember and describe what you saw? Why or why not?

BACKGROUND AND VOCABULARY

1 *Police have new ways to get information about criminals. Read and listen to a conversation between two friends about DNA testing.*

A: Listen to this: "Since 1989, more than 200 people have been let out of **prison** in the United States."

B: Why were they let out?

A: Because they weren't **guilty**. They were in prison for **crimes** they didn't **commit**. They didn't do anything wrong!

B: Really? How did they get out?

A: **DNA** testing.

B: What's that?

A: DNA is information that makes each person different from every other person. It's what decides the color of your eyes, hair, and skin.

B: So, it's what makes me different from you.

A: Yes. And the police can use DNA to find the person who committed a crime.

B: How does that work?

A: Well, we leave DNA everywhere we go; it's in our hair or left when we touch something. When there is a crime, the police can collect **evidence**; something that might help them find who committed the crime. For example, evidence can be a hair or something the person touched, like a can of soda or even the **victim** of the crime. The police test the DNA. Then they use a computer to see if the police found the same DNA at another crime scene. If so, they know who committed the crime and they can **arrest** that person.

B: But how does it help people get out of prison?

A: Now DNA can be used to show people are **innocent**. This happens when the DNA the police get is different than the DNA of the person in prison.

B: So people just leave prison?

A: No, it's not that easy. There's an organization called the Innocence Project that helps people who are in prison **prove** they are innocent. And they have helped more than 200 people in the United States, Canada, England, and Australia.

B: That's great. And this is new?

A: Yes. Before, the police used information from **eyewitnesses**—the people who saw the crime. But eyewitnesses can be wrong. With DNA, the police can prove who committed the crime.

B: That's interesting!

2 *Match the words on the left with the definitions on the right.*

_e_ **1.** prison

_____ **2.** guilty

_____ **3.** crimes

_____ **4.** commit

_____ **5.** DNA

_____ **6.** evidence

_____ **7.** victim

_____ **8.** arrest

_____ **9.** innocent

_____ **10.** prove

_____ **11.** eyewitness

a. do something bad

b. information in the human body that makes each person different from others

c. a person who saw something happen

d. things done against the law

e. a place where people who committed a crime stay

f. not guilty

g. to take a person to a police station

h. to show something is true

i. a person who is hurt by someone

j. information that shows that something is true

k. activities that are against the law

2 FOCUS ON LISTENING

A **LISTENING ONE: Roger's Story**

CD 7
36 *You will listen to a story about Roger—a man who went to prison. It is based on true stories. Listen to the beginning of Roger's story. What do you think he will talk about? Check (✓) everything he might say.*

_____ the reason he was sent to prison

_____ why the police thought he was guilty

_____ what he did in prison

_____ people he met in prison

_____ how he got out of prison

_____ where the prison was located

LISTEN FOR MAIN IDEAS

CD 1
37
*Listen to Roger's whole story. Then read each statement. Write **T** (true) or **F** (false). Correct the false statements.*

_____ 1. Roger spent 25 years in prison.

_____ 2. He was guilty.

_____ 3. He heard about DNA testing before going to prison.

_____ 4. The Innocence Project helped Roger.

LISTEN FOR DETAILS

CD 1
38
Listen to Roger's story again. Fill in the missing information.

1. Roger was living in Chicago in _____.

2. The police showed the victim _____ pictures.

3. In May _____, there was a trial and Roger was found guilty and convicted.

4. The police _____ believe Roger's wife and family.

5. The police _____ the DNA evidence from Roger's case; they could not test it.

6. In _____, Roger heard about the Innocence Project.

7. The Innocence Project worked with the police to _____ the DNA evidence.

8. In _____, Roger walked out of prison. He was a free man.

MAKE INFERENCES

Listen to three excerpts from Roger's story. Then decide whether the person would agree or disagree with the statement. Circle your answer.

CD 1
39
Excerpt One

"The families will always try to protect each other, so they will often lie."

Would the police agree or disagree?

    a. agree   **b.** disagree

CD 1
40
Excerpt Two

"The police did the best they could—they wanted to help prove I was innocent."

Would Roger agree or disagree?

    a. agree   **b.** disagree

(continued on next page)

CD 7
41 **Excerpt Three**

> "I'm not angry at anyone. I understand why they sent me to prison."

Would Roger agree or disagree?

    a. agree   **b.** disagree

Compare your answers with a classmate's. Explain your answers using details from the listening.

◖ **EXPRESS OPINIONS**

*Work with a partner. Read the quotes from people who have just listened to Roger's story. Do you agree or disagree? Write **A** (agree) or **D** (disagree). Discuss your opinions.*

1. "I think what happened to Roger is terrible. I hope the government gives him a lot of money and helps him get a job and a place to live." _____

2. "It's too bad what happened to him. I feel that he should just be happy that he is out of prison and go on with his life." _____

3. "In my opinion, it's a good thing there are organizations like the Innocence Project. I don't know who else could help Roger." _____

4. "I can't believe that the police didn't believe his family. That really surprises me." _____

B **LISTENING TWO: Why Do Innocent People Go to Prison?**

CD 7
42 *Listen to an interview with an Innocence Project lawyer. She explains why innocent people sometimes go to prison. Then answer the questions. You don't need to write complete sentences.*

1. What does Laura Chang do?

  _____

2. What is mistaken identity?

  _____

3. Why does mistaken identity happen? Write one or more reasons.

  _____

4. What is false confession?

  _____

5. Why would someone give a false confession? Write one or more reasons.

  _____

6. What is police misconduct?

_____

7. What is an example of police misconduct?

_____

8. What is an example of a lawyer doing a bad job?

_____

C INTEGRATE LISTENINGS ONE AND TWO

◀ **STEP 1: Organize**

Complete the chart. In the left column, write reasons why innocent people go to prison. In the right column, write examples for each reason from Listenings One and Two.

REASONS WHY INNOCENT PEOPLE GO TO PRISON	EXAMPLES FROM LISTENINGS 1 AND 2
1. mistaken identity	eyewitness was wrong about Roger
2.	
3.	
4.	

◀ **STEP 2: Synthesize**

Work with a partner. Student A, give a reason why innocent people go to prison. Student B, give an example from Listening One or Two. Use the information from Step 1. Then switch roles. Continue until you have talked about all the reasons.

Example

A: One reason innocent people go to prison is mistaken identity.
B: Roger's case is an example of that. The victim was wrong about Roger.

A VOCABULARY

REVIEW

Use the words from the box to complete the sentences.

arrested	false confession	police misconduct
DNA	guilty	prison
evidence	innocent	prove
~~eyewitness~~	mistaken identity	victim

1. A person who sees a crime is a(n) ___eyewitness___.

2. Jerry was home when the police came to his house. They _____ him and took him to the police station.

3. A person can be wrong about what he or she saw. This is called

   _____.

4. Lawyers use _____ to try to show a person committed a crime.

5. _____ is information in a person's body that makes him or her different from everyone else; it determines things like the color of your eyes and hair.

6. A person who did not commit a crime is _____.

7. A person who has committed a crime will be sent to _____.

8. Sometimes a person will say they committed a crime even if they did not. They might feel scared or pressured to give a _____.

9. Sometimes the police will do things wrong, such as destroy evidence. This is one example of _____.

10. Someone stole my sister's car last night. This is the first time anyone in my family has been the _____ of a crime.

11. Lawyers have a hard job; they must _____ if someone did something wrong or not.

12. A person who committed a crime is _____.

1 *Read the frequently asked questions (FAQs) about global DNA databases.*

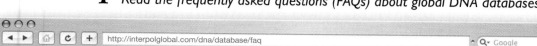

http://interpolglobal.com/dna/database/faq   Q▾ Google

FAQs on Interpol's Global DNA Database

What is Interpol?
Interpol (The International Criminal Police Organization) is the world's largest police organization. It has 186 countries.

What is a global DNA database?
A DNA database is a collection of 64,000 DNA samples taken from people in 42 countries. It is kept in a computer. Police can use the database to find **criminals** in any country.

Why should there be a global DNA database?
A global DNA database can help the police **solve a crime** in any country. It can help the police to quickly match the DNA they found at a **crime scene** with the DNA in the database. DNA can also help people **prove their innocence**.

Who should give a DNA sample?
One way is to ask everyone to give a DNA sample. Another idea is to take DNA when the police arrest someone. The third way is to take DNA only from people who are **found guilty** and sent to prison.

2 *Read each statement. Then circle the correct definition of the underlined word.*

1. The police arrived at the <u>crime scene</u> and found the victim. She was sitting on the ground and very scared.
   - **a.** the place something bad happened
   - **b.** the police station

2. The global DNA database can help the police find <u>criminals</u> in any country.
   - **a.** people who commit crimes
   - **b.** people who didn't do anything wrong

3. The eyewitness told the lawyers what she saw. The lawyers used her information and other evidence in court. The man who committed the crime was <u>found guilty</u>.
   - **a.** someone decided the person committed the crime
   - **b.** someone decided the person did not commit the crime

(continued on next page)

4. DNA evidence can help people <u>prove their innocence</u>.

    a. show they didn't commit the crime   **b.** commit crimes

5. The police can use DNA evidence and eyewitnesses' stories to <u>solve crimes</u>.

    a. understand crimes   **b.** find the people who committed
                              the crimes

◖ CREATE

Work with a partner. Student A, you were arrested, found guilty, and put in prison, but you are innocent. Student B, interview Student A. Find out what happened. Then switch roles. Use the questions on this page and vocabulary from Review and Expand.

Example

B: When did the police arrest you?

A: They arrested me last year.

B: Were there any eyewitnesses?

A: There was an eyewitness but I think she made a mistake. It was too dark. She couldn't see well but the police believed her anyway.

Questions

When did the police arrest you?

Where was the crime scene?

Was there evidence or an eyewitness?

Why do you think they found you guilty?

Can you prove your innocence? How?

1 *Read the questions and answers.*

Did the people at the Innocence Project help Roger?	Yes, they did.
Did Roger stay in prison?	No, he didn't.
Was Roger innocent?	Yes, he was.
Were the police helpful?	No, they weren't.
When did Roger get out of prison?	He got out two years ago.
Where did he go?	He went home.
Who helped Roger?	The Innocence Project helped him.

2 *Answer the questions.*

    a. What is the verb in each question or answer?

    b. What form is the main verb in each question or answer?

    c. What form are the other verbs?

THE SIMPLE PAST: *YES / NO* AND *WH-* QUESTIONS

1. *Yes / No* questions in the simple past have the same form (***Did + subject + base form***) for regular and irregular verbs.	**Did** you **commit** a crime? [regular verb] **Did** she **write** to the [irregular verb] Innocence Project?	No, I didn't. Yes, she did.
Yes / No questions with ***be*** are formed by putting ***was*** or ***were*** before the subject.	**Was** he innocent? **Were** you in prison?	Yes, he was. Yes, I was.
2. Most *wh-* questions in the past begin with the **question word** followed by ***did + subject + the base form*** of the verb.	**When did** he **go** to prison? **Where did** he **live**? **What did** the police **do**? **Why did** he **go** to prison? **How long did** he **stay** in prison?	He went to prison in 1975. He lived in New York. They lost the evidence. He committed a crime. He stayed in prison for 22 years.
Wh- questions in the past do not use *did* when the question is about the subject.	**Who** helped? (Not: Who did help?)	The Innocence Project helped.

(continued on next page)

3. There are three endings for regular verbs in the simple past: **-d, -ed** and **-ied**.

Irregular past verbs do not add *–ed*.
They often look different from the base form.

Roger **lived** in Chicago.
The police **talked** to the victim.
The lawyers **tried** to help Roger.

The eyewitness **saw** the crime.
Roger's family **went** to the movies.

3 *Write the verbs in the past tense.*

Base Form	Past Tense	Base Form	Past Tense
accuse	_____	help	_____
arrest	_____	leave	_____
be	_____	live	_____
come	_____	prove	_____
commit	_____	say	_____
die	_____	see	_____
do	_____	take	_____
find	_____	tell	_____
go	_____	test	_____
have	_____	write	_____

4 *Look at the timeline of events in Jack Smith's life. He was arrested, but he wasn't guilty. Work with a partner. Take turns asking and answering questions about the events.*

Example

A: Where did Jack live in 2000?
B: He lived in New York City.
B: What happened on March 18?
A: He had an accident.

Name: Jack Smith
Hometown: New York City

| March 18, 2000 | January 2001 | December 2003 | January 2005 |

- is in his car with his friend, John
- has an accident and John dies
- Jack hits his head and can't remember accident
- an eyewitness sees the accident; says Jack was the driver
- police arrest Jack because his friend dies

- has trial
- found guilty
- goes to prison

- remembers what happened
- writes to Innocence Project
- DNA tests prove Jack wasn't the driver

- has new trial
- the lawyer uses DNA evidence
- Jack found not guilty
- leaves prison

C SPEAKING

◖ PRONUNCIATION: *–ed* Endings—A Sound or a Syllable?

Sometimes the –ed ending is pronounced as a new syllable. Sometimes it is pronounced as a single sound at the end of the verb. Listen to the underlined words in the text.

🔊 43 The Innocence Project <u>decided</u> to look at Roger Brook's case. They <u>investigated</u> and <u>helped</u> Roger prove that he was innocent. Roger's family never <u>believed</u> that he was guilty. Finally, after 25 years, the court <u>agreed</u> with Roger and his family.

Write the verbs from the text in the correct blanks.

The *–ed* ending is pronounced as a syllable: _____

The *–ed* ending is pronounced as a single, final sound: _____

_____

RULES FOR PRONOUNCING THE –ED ENDING

The –ed ending is a syllable when the verb ends in a /t/ or /d/ sound. The –ed ending is pronounced /ɪd/.	decide–decid<u>ed</u> investigate–investigat<u>ed</u>
The –ed ending is a final sound, /t/, when the verb ends in a voiceless sound.	work—wor<u>ked</u> help—hel<u>ped</u> /k/ /kt/ /p/ /pt/ release—relea<u>sed</u> laugh—lau<u>ghed</u> /s/ /st/ /f/ /ft/
The –ed ending is a final sound, /d/, when the verb ends in a voiced sound or a vowel sound.	agree—agree<u>d</u> believe—belie<u>ved</u> /d/ /v/ /vd/

1 *Write the verbs in the correct column. Check your answers with a partner's and practice saying the verbs aloud.*

arrested	listened	married	tried
convicted	lived	recommended	wanted
ended	located	started	watched
happened	loved	tested	worked

-ed is a syllable

_____

_____

_____

_____

_____

_____

_____

-ed is a sound

_____

_____

_____

_____

_____

_____

_____

2 Work with a partner. Write the past tense of the verb in the correct column. Then put the sentences in the correct order to tell Roger Brook's story. Practice telling the story to a partner.

ORDER	STORY	IRREGULAR VERB	–ED IS A SYLLABLE	–ED IS A SOUND
	The court (review) the new evidence.			
	The police (show) the victim pictures of suspects.			
1	In 1980, someone (commit) a crime.		committed	
	The police (arrest) Roger.			
	Roger (go) to prison.			
	The victim (pick) Roger's picture.			
	Roger (write) a letter to the Innocence Project about his case in prison.			
	The police (find) the DNA evidence.			
	Roger was (convict) of the crime.			
	Roger (walk) out of prison a free man.			
	The DNA evidence (prove) that Roger was innocent.			

◀ FUNCTION: Expressing and Supporting an Opinion

Often in conversation, we want to express opinions on a topic. An opinion is something you believe to be true. Different people can have different opinions about the same thing. To get other people to agree with you, you should give reasons to support your opinion. You should say why you believe your opinion is true.

EXPRESSING AND SUPPORTING AN OPINION	AGREEING WITH AN OPINION	DISAGREEING WITH AN OPINION
I think DNA databases are a good idea [expressing opinion] because they help the police. [supporting an opinion] I feel that . . . In my opinion, . . . I believe . . . I don't think we should have DNA databases [expressing opinion] because DNA information should be private. [supporting an opinion] I don't feel . . . I don't believe . . .	I think so, too. I agree.	I don't think so. I don't agree. I disagree.

Work in a small group. One student reads a statement. Each student agrees or disagrees with the statement and explains his or her opinion.

Example

DNA databases are a good idea.

A: In my opinion, DNA databases are a good idea because they help solve crimes.
B: I disagree. I don't think DNA databases are a good idea. I think DNA information should be private.

1. The Innocence Project should help everyone in prison.

2. Everyone should give a DNA sample to a global DNA database.

3. A person who sees a crime is always a good eyewitness.

4. The police never do anything wrong.

5. A person in prison is there because he or she committed a crime.

6. The government should give people like Roger a lot of money.

Every day, the Innocence Project lawyers receive many letters from people in prison. These prisoners want the Innocence Project to help them prove they are innocent. The Innocence Project lawyers cannot take every case, but they take as many as possible. ***Imagine that you are working for the Innocence Project and have to choose the cases that you can help.*** Try to use the vocabulary, grammar, pronunciation, and language for expressing and supporting opinions that you learned in the unit.*

Work in a group of three. Each student has information on one case. Student A, your chart is on page 183. Student B, your chart is on page 184, and Student C, your chart is on page 185. Follow the steps.

Step 1: Before you decide on the cases, each student in the group must know about all the cases. Take turns asking each other questions about the cases until your charts are complete.

Example

A: How old is Louis Silver?
B: He is 53 years old.

B: Where did Dan Block live?
C: He lived in Chicago.

Step 2: When you all have complete information on each case, decide which case the Innocence Project will take first, second, and third. You must give your opinion and reasons why you think one case should be taken before another.

Example

A: I think we should take Johnny Muldar first. He was at home when the crime happened.
B: I don't think we should take his case first. We should take Dan Block's case first because he gave a false confession. He was probably very scared and didn't know what to do.

Step 3: After you decide the order of the cases, tell the class what order you recommend and why.

*For Alternative Speaking Topics, see page 72.

Listening Activity

Complete the chart with each group's choice of cases. Put a check (✓) under first, second, and third for each group's decision. What were the class's overall results?

	JOHNNY MULDAR	LOUIS SILVER	DAN BLOCK
First			
Second			
Third			

ALTERNATIVE SPEAKING TOPICS

Work in a small group. Discuss the questions.

1. How do you think innocent people can be protected from going to prison?

2. Imagine a person has been in prison for 20 years. Then, this person gets out because of DNA evidence. What kind of problems do you think this person faces? Make a list of needs a person might have. Explain each need.

RESEARCH TOPICS, see page 190.

Etiquette

1 FOCUS ON THE TOPIC

A PREDICT

Look at the picture and discuss the questions with the class.

1. What is happening?

2. Have you been in a similar situation? What happened? How did you feel?

73

Look at the list of actions. Some are polite (make other people feel comfortable); others are rude (make others feel uncomfortable). For each action, circle a number from **1** to **4** to express your opinion. Be prepared to explain your opinions.

	VERY POLITE			VERY RUDE
1. holding the door open for someone else to walk through	1	2	3	4
2. pointing at someone	1	2	3	4
3. taking your shoes off before entering a house	1	2	3	4
4. staring at someone	1	2	3	4
5. eating while walking down the street	1	2	3	4
6. helping someone who dropped something	1	2	3	4
7. putting on makeup in public	1	2	3	4
8. talking on a cell phone while in a restaurant with friends	1	2	3	4
9. not looking at your teacher when speaking or answering	1	2	3	4
10. throwing garbage on the ground (littering)	1	2	3	4

Why are some of the actions considered polite? Why are some considered rude? Discuss your opinions with the class.

1 $\overset{C D 7}{\textbf{44}}$ *Read and listen to an excerpt from a radio show.*

HOST: Thanks for tuning into *Your World*. At the end of every show, we ask you to tell us what you'd like to hear about on this radio station. Several listeners wrote in saying they'd like to hear about **manners**.

Maybe, like me, you were **raised** by your parents to be **courteous**. My mother always said, "**Treat** others as you want them to treat you." In other words, **respect** others. Many cultures have the same idea. In English, this is called "the golden rule."

On today's show our guest is a woman who just did an international survey[1] on polite and impolite behavior. She sees people being **rude** more often than before. She also hears more and more people **complaining** about bad manners. Please listen at 4:00 P.M. today to another show, *What Ever Happened to Manners?*

2 *Match the words on the left with the definitions on the right.*

   _b_   **1.** manners

         2. raised

         3. courteous

         4. treat

         5. respect

         6. rude

         7. complaining

a. speaking or doing things in a way that is not polite

b. polite ways to behave or speak; polite social behavior

c. taken care of as a child

d. to behave toward someone in a particular way

e. saying you are unhappy or angry with something or someone

f. a way to describe polite behavior

g. feel or show care for or attention to something

---

[1]**survey:** a set of questions you ask a large number of people to learn their opinions or behavior

②FOCUS ON LISTENING

A LISTENING ONE: What Ever Happened to Manners?

CD 7
45 *Listen to the beginning of the radio show called* What Ever Happened to Manners? *How do you think Sarah Jones did an international survey of manners? List three possible ways.*

1. _____

2. _____

3. _____

◖LISTEN FOR MAIN IDEAS

CD 7
46 *Listen to the complete interview. Then read each question and circle the correct answer.*

1. Why did Sarah Jones do a survey of manners?
   a. She wanted to see if people in one country are more polite than in other countries.
   b. She wanted to see if it is true that people are becoming very rude.
   c. She wanted to see if women are more polite than men.

2. Who did the woman test?
   a. all kinds of people
   b. students and businesspeople
   c. only students

3. What situations were included in the survey?
   a. holding the door for someone, helping someone pick up some papers, and letting someone sit down
   b. helping someone pick up some papers, helping someone cross the street, and customer service
   c. holding the door for someone, helping someone pick up some papers, and customer service

◖LISTEN FOR DETAILS

CD 7
47 *Listen to the interview again. Then complete the summary of the survey that Sarah Jones did.*

_____ reporters went to large cities all around the world. They went
      1.

to _____ countries. In the survey, they tested _____
         2.   3.

people. The reporters did three things: _____, the paper drop test,
                                                    4.

and they looked at _____.
                          5.

For the door test, they wanted to see if people would _____ for the
6.
reporters. For the _____, they wanted to see if anyone would help
7.
them pick up _____. For customer service, they wanted to see if
8.
people who work in stores were polite: if people did courteous things like saying

_____ and _____.
9.   10.

In the most courteous city, _____ percent of the people passed the door
11.
test. When the reporters dropped their papers, only _____ percent
12.
helped pick them up. For customer service, _____ out of 20 people said
13.
"thank-you." When the reporters asked them, some people said they do it because it

shows _____. _____ was the most courteous city.
14.   15.

◖ MAKE INFERENCES

*Listen to two excerpts from the interview. After listening to each excerpt, read the
question and circle the correct answer.*

CD 7
48 **Excerpt One**

Why does Sarah Jones stress the word *her*?

a. to show the person was a woman

b. to show that the woman needed help more than the reporter did

CD 7
49 **Excerpt Two**

Why does Sarah Jones stress the word *are*?

a. She agrees they are courteous because they are being paid.

b. She thinks they have good training.

◖ EXPRESS OPINIONS

Discuss the questions with the class.

1. New York City scored as the number one city for good manners. Are you
   surprised? Why or why not?

2. In your opinion, are people less polite nowadays than in the past? Give
   examples to explain your opinion.

3. Where did you learn manners: At home? At school? At a religious institution?

4. Why are manners important?

LISTENING TWO: Our Listeners Respond—Why Is There a Lack of Manners?

🎧 *Listen to the second part of the radio show. Listeners were invited to call in with their ideas on why people are rude. Look at the list of reasons. Check (✓) the reasons you hear.*

There is a lack of manners because . . .

_____ families don't spend enough time together.

_____ people don't know each other well, so they are less polite.

_____ children don't learn manners at school anymore.

_____ living with people from many different cultures is confusing.

_____ of technology. (People don't socialize as much.)

_____ people follow the behavior they see on TV.

_____ people forget how to talk to someone face to face.

C INTEGRATE LISTENINGS ONE AND TWO

◀ STEP 1: Organize

Look at the list of items from Listenings One and Two. Each item belongs to one of the three categories in the chart on page 79. Categorize each item and write it in the correct column. Then compare your completed chart with a partner's.

- help someone pick up dropped papers
- ~~hold the door for someone~~
- how we want other people to treat us
- how you were raised
- living with many cultures

- ~~not having enough family time~~
- ~~respect for other people~~
- say "thank-you" and "hello"
- technology
- you don't know how long to hold the door
- you're opening the door anyway

EXAMPLES OF COURTEOUS BEHAVIOR	REASONS FOR COURTEOUS BEHAVIOR	REASONS FOR IMPOLITE BEHAVIOR
1. hold the door for someone	1. respect for other people	1. not having enough family time
2.	2.	2.
3.	3.	3.
	4.	4.

◀ **STEP 2: Synthesize**

Work with a partner. Student A, you are a reporter interviewing people on the street about manners. Ask questions. Student B, answer Student A's questions. Use the information from Step 1. Then switch roles and repeat the conversation.

Example

A: Hello. I'm interviewing people about manners. Can you give me an example of courteous behavior?

B: Sure. It is polite to hold the door for someone.

A: True. Why do people do that?

B: It shows respect for other people.

A: But some people aren't courteous. Why is that?

B: One reason is not having enough family time, so children don't learn manners from their parents.

A VOCABULARY

◗ **REVIEW**

Read the magazine column about etiquette. Write the correct word in the blank. Use the words from the box.

complaining	courteous	raised	rude
confusing	face to face	respect	treat

Ask Miss Manners

Dear Miss Manners,

I think people are not as polite now as they used to be. It seems that every day someone gets in front of me in line or bumps into me and doesn't say "excuse me." People are just not _____.
1.
I want to say something to each and every one of them, but I don't. What do you suggest I do?

— **Clara**

Dear Clara,

Unfortunately, there does seem to be a lack of manners. The question is, what do we do about it? I think the important thing to remember is to

_____ others in a nice way. If we can all
2.
just remember to _____ each other, I think
3.
we can all get along.

• • • • • • • • • • • • • • • • • • • •

Dear Miss Manners,

I hear people _____ about parents not
4.
watching their children. I know children are all

_____ differently, so you see a lot of
5.

different behavior. I was shopping the other day and some kids were running around. It was hard to shop. What should I do in that situation?

—**Annoyed Shopper**

Dear Annoyed Shopper,

Well, one idea is to tell the manager. It's really the manager's job to deal with customers. It's not always best for you to talk to the person

_____.
6.

• • • • • • • • • • • • • • • • • • • •

Dear Miss Manners,

Sometimes I feel people from other countries are being _____ because they talk so loud.
7.
What do you suggest I do?

—**Julius K.**

Dear Julius K.,

Nowadays, we live with people from all over the world. We don't always speak the same language or have the same culture. It can be _____
8.
when we don't understand another person's culture. But we all have to learn to get along.

1 C D 7 *Read and listen to the conversation about bad manners on the road. Take turns*
   51 *reading the conversation with a partner.*

   A: I had a terrible day today.
   B: Really? What happened?
   A: Well, first I was driving to school, and a man drove right in front of me really
      fast. I had to slam on my brakes to stop quickly.
   B: Oh, **don't take it personally** . . . I'm sure he didn't even see you there!
   A: Well, then, I was late and in a hurry and he was driving too slowly.
   B: Maybe he was trying to be careful. **Try to see it his way**. I'm sure it had nothing
      to do with you.
   A: Then why didn't he pull over and let me go?
   B: **Don't get me wrong**. I understand why you're angry, but I think you're thinking
      too much about this whole thing. Just forget it.
   A: Forget it? I can't! I got to school late and missed my test.
   B: Hey, **take it easy** . . . you're so upset! If you leave home a little earlier, then you
      won't be late.
   A: Well, good point.

2 *Match the phrases on the left with their meaning on the right.*

   _____ **1.** don't take it personally   **a.** try to understand what I am (he / she
                                                          is) thinking
   _____ **2.** try to see it my / her /
             his way   **b.** stop being angry; don't worry, relax

   _____ **3.** don't get me wrong   **c.** don't misunderstand me

   _____ **4.** take it easy   **d.** what I am saying or what happened is
                                                          not about you

◀ **CREATE**

*Work in a group of four. You will have a debate about each of the actions listed. For
each action, each student will take a side—either you think it is rude or not. Use the
words from the box and vocabulary from Review and Expand in your statements.*

Actions

Walking down the street while eating   Talking on your cell phone in public

Crossing your legs on the subway   Pointing at people

Putting on makeup in public

confusing	lack of manners	raised	rude
courteous	polite	respect	treat

Example

A: I think walking down the street while eating is rude. I think when you eat you sit and enjoy the food. That is how I was raised.

B: I disagree. Maybe you don't have time to sit and eat and you are very hungry. It's not a lack of manners.

C: Don't get me wrong. Sometimes I walk and eat, but I think it shows respect to sit down to a meal.

B GRAMMAR: *Could* and *Would* in Polite Questions

1 *Read the examples. Then answer the questions.*

Could you please hold the door open for me?

Would you help me pick up my papers?

Could you help me, please?

a. What is the first word in each question? What answer do you expect?

b. Look at the main verb in each question. What is the form?

COULD AND WOULD IN POLITE QUESTIONS

1. Use **could** and **would** when you want to make a polite request or politely ask someone for something. **Could** and **would** have the same meaning. *Could* and *would* are modals. The verb that follows *could* and *would* is in the simple form.	**Could** you **hold** the door for me? **Would** you **help** me with the dishes?
2. *Please* is often used to make the question even more polite.	Could you **please** hold the door for me? Would you help me with the dishes, **please**?
3. To answer politely, use these typical responses:	Yes, of course. Certainly. I'd be glad to. I'd be happy to. Sure. No problem.

2 *Work with a partner. Student A and Student B, you have incomplete schedules for the etiquette school—a school that teaches manners to business people. Student A, your schedule is on this page. Student B, turn to page 186. Take turns asking and answering questions until you both have a complete schedule.*

Example

A: Could you tell me when the class "Telephone Etiquette" meets?
B: I'd be glad to. It meets Thursdays, 6–7.
A: And could you tell me a little about the class?
B: Sure. You will learn how to answer the phone politely.
A: What else?

Student A, ask Student B about these classes. Write them in your schedule.

Social and Communication Skills   Business Meals

Telephone Etiquette

	Monday	Tuesday	Wednesday	Thursday	Friday
6–7			**How to Make a Toast** Learn: • the right time to make a toast • what to say • how to hold the glass • how long to talk	Telephone Etiquette Learn: • to answer the phone politely • •	
7–8	**Business Communication** Learn: • how to greet people from different countries • when to make eye contact • how to exchange business cards • how to dress correctly for meetings				**Table Manners** Learn: • styles of eating in different countries • how to understand table settings • how to eat unusual food • when to begin eating
8–9					

◀ PRONUNCIATION: Intonation: Attention Getters and Polite Questions

When we want to get someone's attention, we can say "Excuse me" or "Sorry." When we say "Sorry" to get someone's attention, we are saying, "I'm sorry if I am interrupting you, but I need to talk to you." We can also get a person's attention by saying the person's name, "Sonia," "Mr. Smith." With strangers, we can say "Sir," "Miss," or "Ma'am" (*Ma'am* / mæm / rhymes with "ham"). We use a special intonation with attention getters like "Excuse me" or "Mr. Jones."

🔊 *CD 7 52 Listen to the attention getters.*

Excuse me, . . .   Sir, . . .

Sorry, . . .   Mr. Smith, ...

Listen to the attention getters again. At the end of the attention getter, does the voice fall to a low note or does it stay a little high?

When we ask polite questions, we use a special intonation.

🔊 *CD 7 52 Listen to the questions.*

Do you have the time?

Can you hold the door for me?

Would you like me to hold the door for you?

1 *CD 7 53 With polite questions, the speaker's voice falls to a low note and then rises to a high note at the end. Listen to the questions again. Underline the word(s) where the voice falls to a low note and then rises to a high note.*

INTONATION PATTERNS	
Attention getters Your voice rises a little at the end.	Excuse me, . . . Miss, . . .
Polite questions Your voice falls to a low note on the important word and then continues to rise to a high note. The important part of the intonation pattern is the fall to the low note and then the rise to a high note.	Do you have the time? Can you hold the door for me?
Attention getters and polite questions together	Excuse me, do you have the time? Sonia, can you hold the door for me?

2 C D 7 *Listen to the questions. Underline the part of the question where the voice falls and then rises. Then listen again and repeat the questions.*

    1. Can you help me?

    2. Could you turn off your cell phone?

    3. Can I ask you a question?

    4. Could you help me with some directions?

    5. Would you like some help?

    6. Is this seat taken?*

    7. You look lost. Can I help you?

    8. Can I borrow your book?

3 C D 7 / 55 *Listen to the attention getters and repeat them. Make your voice rise at the end.*

    1. Excuse me, . . .

    2. Sir, . . .

    3. Carlos, . . .

    4. Sorry, . . .

    5. Ma'am, . . .

    6. Mrs. Peters, . . .

    7. Professor Jones, . . .

    8. Dr. Sanford, . . .

4 *Work with a partner. Practice putting the attention getters together with a polite question. Pay attention to your intonation.*

5 *Practice the short conversations with a partner.*

    1. **A:** Excuse me, do you have the time?
       B: Sure. It's 10:30.

    2. **A:** Sonia, can I borrow your book?
       B: No problem.

    3. **A:** Sir, is this seat taken?
       B: No.

    4. **A:** Ma'am, could you get that door for me?
       B: Sure. You've got quite an armful.

---

*You can use this question when there is an empty seat next to someone who is sitting.

6 *Create short conversations with your partner about the situations below. Student A, start with an attention getter and a polite question. Student B, answer the question. Then repeat the exercise, switching roles. You can use the attention getters and questions from the exercises on page 85 or make your own.*

1. You are walking down the street. A person in front of you drops some papers. The person is trying to pick them up. You ask if you can help.

2. You need to make a call but you don't have your cell phone with you. You ask a classmate if you can borrow his or her cell phone.

3. You're carrying a lot of heavy packages. The person in front of you is opening the door. You ask if he or she can hold the door for you.

4. You've lost your class schedule. You ask your teacher if you can get another one.

5. You see someone on the street who looks lost. You ask if you can help.

6. You were absent and want to get the notes from yesterday's class. You ask a classmate if you can borrow his or her notes.

◖ **FUNCTION: Complaining Politely**

There are different ways to complain politely when you are not happy about a situation.

MAKING POLITE COMPLAINTS	RESPONSES
I'm sorry to have to say this, but . . .	I can see why you are upset.
I'm sorry to bother you, but . . .	No problem.
Maybe you forgot to . . .	I'm sorry.
Maybe you didn't know, but . . .	Let me see what I can do.
Excuse me if I'm out of line, but . . .	

Work with a partner. Act out the situations. Use the language for making polite complaints. Then repeat the exercise, switching roles.

1. Student A: You drop some garbage on the ground.

   Student B: You see Student A litter and don't think it is right.

2. Student A: You like people to take their shoes off before entering your home.

   Student B: You are visiting Student A. You don't take your shoes off before entering the home.

3. **Student A:** You are in a movie theater, watching a movie. Student B is talking to friends and it bothers you.

   Student B: You are talking to your friends during the movie.

4. **Student A:** You are sending text messages to another friend while Student B is trying to talk to you.

   Student B: You are trying to have a conversation with Student A.

◀ PRODUCTION: Role Play

In this activity, you will *discuss a situation, then prepare a three-to-five-minute role play that relates to manners*. A role play is a short performance. The actors take on roles, or become characters, and act out a situation. The situations are often similar to experiences that people might have in real life. Try to use the vocabulary, grammar, pronunciation, and language for making polite complaints that you learned in the unit.*

Work in a group of three. Follow the steps.

Step 1: Read each situation aloud in your group. Discuss the situations. What was rude? Why was it rude? How could you react? What could you say? What might happen if you say something?

Situations

1. You are in a restaurant having dinner with a friend. A person is sitting alone at a table near you, talking loudly on a cell phone. You can't hear your friend or enjoy your meal.

2. You are in the grocery store, standing in line to pay for your groceries. You are in a hurry to go to a friend's house. The person in line in front of you and the cashier are having a long conversation.

3. You are at the movies with a friend. It is a new movie and very popular. The line is long and you don't know if you will get tickets. Someone has been standing in line in front of you alone. Suddenly, three of his friends come and get in line in front of you and your friend.

4. You are driving with your friend. Another car comes close behind you, quickly passes, then drives very closely in front of you. A few minutes later, you stop to buy a cup of coffee. You go into the restaurant, look out the window, and see the same car stop as well. The driver comes into the restaurant.

---

*For Alternative Speaking Topics, see page 88.

Step 2: Choose one situation and prepare a role play.

Step 3: Role-play your situation for the class.

Listening Activity

Complete the chart for each group's role play.

SITUATION	RESPONSE	DO YOU AGREE WITH THE RESPONSE? WHY?

ALTERNATIVE SPEAKING TOPICS

Work in a small group. Read and discuss the quotes. What do they mean to you? Explain each quote in your own words. Do you agree or disagree with the quote? Explain.

"Treat everyone with politeness, even those who are rude to you—not because they are nice, but because you are."—Author Unknown

"Consideration for others is the basis of a good life, a good society."—Confucius

"Visitors should behave in such a way that the host and hostess feel at home." —J.S. Farynski

RESEARCH TOPICS, see page 190.

UNIT 6

Who's Game for These Games?

1 FOCUS ON THE TOPIC

A PREDICT

Look at the pictures and discuss the questions with the class.

1. Where are the people in the pictures?

2. What are they doing?

3. Which picture shows someone playing a computer game? An arcade game? A video game? What games do you think they are playing?

4. Read the title of the unit. The expression *to be game* means "to be ready and willing to do something," so the title means "who is ready and willing to play these games?" Who do you think plays video and computer games?

89

1 What things are important when you choose a game to play? Check (✓) **Important** or **Not Very Important**. You can think of an electronic (video or computer) game or another kind of game.

	IMPORTANT	NOT VERY IMPORTANT
1. It's challenging (it's difficult to win).		
2. It's exciting.	✓	
3. It has an interesting story.		✓
4. It's funny (it makes me laugh).		
5. It's educational (it teaches me something).	✓	✓
6. It's active (I can move around when I play).	✓	✓
7. I can play it with other people.	✓	
8. I can play it alone.	✓	

2 Discuss your answers in a small group. Tell why each item is important or not important to you. Give some examples of games that you know.

3 Study the graphs and discuss the questions on page 91 with your group.

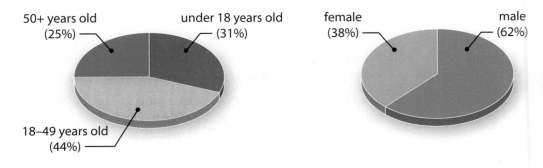

Age of Game Players (The average age is 33.)

50+ years old (25%)
under 18 years old (31%)
18–49 years old (44%)

Gender of Game Players

female (38%)
male (62%)

1. What is the average age of computer and video game players?

2. Are more players male or female?

3. Does any of the information in the graphs surprise you? Why?

4. Are you a gamer (someone who plays video or computer games)?

C BACKGROUND AND VOCABULARY

1 ^{CD2} **2** *Read and listen to the article from a parenting magazine.*

HOW MUCH DO YOU KNOW ABOUT YOUR KIDS' GAMES?

As a parent, you probably know that video and computer games are very popular with children: 83 percent of 8-to-18-year-olds in the United States have at least one video game system in their home. However, maybe you don't know much about the games your kids are playing. Here are some popular types of electronic games:

Role-playing: These games take place in a **(1) fantasy** world. Players take the role of a character, or create their own character. Many people play these games online.

Action-Adventure: These games are very popular with children because they are fast-moving and full of **(2) adventure**. In these games, players **(3) explore** the fantasy world of the game. To win the game, players have different challenges, such as solving **(4) puzzles**, winning races, searching for treasures, and fighting battles against monsters.

Shooting: In these games, players use weapons, such as guns, to shoot other characters in the game. Players often fight against each other.

Simulation: In these games, players can simulate or re-create real situations, such as flying an airplane or a spaceship. In some simulation games, players create their own cities, countries, families, or even zoos, and act as the planner or leader to meet the needs of the game characters.

In many games, players use weapons to battle monsters or other characters.

Many parents think that video games are bad for their children. For example, many people think that some games are too **(5) violent** and they teach kids to be violent or hurt others. Some parents worry that their children will **(6) get addicted to** video games and spend too much time playing games instead of doing other things. On the other hand, there are some good things about games. The quick movements of video games can help children develop good hand-eye **(7) coordination**, and some games help children learn to think and solve problems. As a parent, it's a good idea to **(8) check out** the games your children play to make sure they aren't too violent. It's also important to limit the time your children spend playing games.

2 *Match the words and phrases on the left with the definitions on the right.*

   f   **1.** fantasy   **a.** games that are difficult to do or solve

   c   **2.** adventure   **b.** become unable to stop doing something

   h   **3.** explore   **c.** an exciting thing that happens to someone

   a   **4.** puzzles   **d.** the way body parts work together

   g   **5.** violent   **e.** examine

   b   **6.** get addicted to   **f.** something imagined

   d   **7.** coordination   **g.** using force to hurt someone

   e   **8.** check out   **h.** learn about a place by traveling through it

②FOCUS ON LISTENING

Ⓐ LISTENING ONE: Entertainment for All

Video and computer games are big business. Many companies make the games and try to get new groups of people to buy them. One way they advertise new games is through expositions, or expos.

1 CD 2 *Listen to the beginning of* Entertainment for All. *Read each question. Then circle the correct answer.*

1. What are you listening to?
   - **a.** a television news report
   - **b.** a conversation
   - **c.** an advertisement

2. Where is reporter Michelle Singh?
   - **a.** at an electronic gaming company
   - **b.** at a party for gamers
   - **c.** at an electronic games expo

At a gaming exposition (expo)

2 *Make predictions about the gaming expo. Circle all the items that are correct.*

Visitors to this gaming expo can . . .

a. check out the latest electronic games.

b. see a gaming competition.

c. sell their used games.

d. see a video game rock concert.

◖ LISTEN FOR MAIN IDEAS

CD 2
4 *You will hear a father, son, and grandfather talk about the kinds of games they like to play. Write the letter next to each person.*

___d___ **Father**

___a___ **Son**

___e___ **Grandfather**

a. Action-adventure
b. Shooting
c. Music and Rhythm
d. Role-playing
e. Puzzle
f. Simulation

◖ LISTEN FOR DETAILS

CD 2
5 *Listen to the complete news story again. What does each person say about his favorite game? Put a check (✓) under the person.*

WHAT DOES EACH PERSON SAY ABOUT HIS FAVORITE GAME(S)?	FATHER	SON	GRANDFATHER
1. You play in a fantasy world.	✓		
2. You create your own character.	✓	✓	
3. You fight battles.	✓		
4. You meet other players.	✓		
5. It's exciting.		✓	
6. You explore.		✓	
7. You solve puzzles.	✓		✓
8. It's challenging.		✓	
9. It's good for your coordination.			✓
10. It makes you think.	✓		✓

Now go back to Section 2A, Exercise 2 on page 92. Were your predictions correct?

Who's Game for These Games?   **93**

◖ MAKE INFERENCES

Listen to three excerpts from the news reports. After each excerpt, circle the correct answers.

CD 2 **6** Excerpt One

1. "Gamers are usually young."
   Would the reporter agree or disagree?

   a. agree   **b.** disagree

2. Why does the man say "actually . . ."?

   a. He wants to correct the reporter.
   b. He wants the reporter to know he's telling the truth.

CD 2 **7** Excerpt Two

1. "It's strange for a man to create a female character in a game."
   Would the reporter agree or disagree?

   a. agree   **b.** disagree

2. What does the reporter mean when she says "what do you know"?

   a. She doesn't think the man knows what he's talking about.
   b. She is surprised that most men create female characters.

CD 2 **8** Excerpt Three

1. "My favorite game isn't very violent."
   Would the boy agree or disagree?

   a. agree   **b.** disagree

2. Why does the reporter say "don't you think"?

   a. She expects the boy to agree with her.
   b. The boy doesn't think enough about the games he plays.

Compare your answers with a classmate's. Explain your answers using details from the listening.

◖ EXPRESS OPINIONS

Read the statements and circle if you agree or disagree. Then discuss your answers in a small group.

1. In my country, most children play video or computer games.	agree	disagree
2. Video games are bad for children.	agree	disagree
3. In my country, more males than females play video games.	agree	disagree
4. I don't know many adults who play video games.	agree	disagree
5. I think video games can keep your mind young.	agree	disagree

LISTENING TWO: Do You Like Video Games, Too?

🎵 CD 2
9

*Listen to the conversation between neighbors. Two mothers and a daughter are talking about electronic games. Write **T** (true) or **F** (false) next to each statement. Correct the false statements.*

_____ **1.** Maria likes her son's video games.

_____ **2.** Jessica and Kelly both like to play video games.

_____ **3.** Jessica plays a simulation game called the Sims.™

_____ **4.** In Jessica's favorite game, she designed a house with a swimming pool.

_____ **5.** Jessica likes games that are easy to win.

_____ **6.** Kelly's favorite game is a karaoke game.

_____ **7.** Kelly likes her dancing game because it's active.

C   INTEGRATE LISTENINGS ONE AND TWO

◀ STEP 1: Organize

Work with a partner. In the chart, write the things the game players like about the games they play. Use the information from Listenings One and Two.

FAVORITE GAME TYPE	WHAT THE PLAYERS LIKE ABOUT THEIR FAVORITE GAME(S)
Online Role-Playing	You can play in a fantasy world.
Action-Adventure	
Puzzle	
Simulation	
Music and Rhythm	

Work in a small group. Imagine you are at a gaming expo. Take turns asking and answering questions about the different types of games you like to play. Use the information from Step 1.

Example

A: What kind of games do you like to play?
B: I like online role-playing games.
A: What do you like about them?
B: I like playing in a fantasy world. I also like to create my own character.

(3) FOCUS ON SPEAKING

A VOCABULARY

REVIEW

1 *Do you like solving puzzles? Make words from the scrambled letters. Write one letter in each square to spell a word or phrase from the word box. Don't worry yet about the numbers below the boxes. You will use them in the next exercise.*

active	fantasy	puzzles
challenging	gamers	use weapons
coordination	get addicted to	~~violent~~

1. Many parents say that games are too TLENOVI and have too much fighting in them.

| V | I | O | L | E | N | T |

     1

2. They don't want their children to play games that teach them to EUS PWEOSAN to kill other characters.

| u | s | e | | w | e | a | p | o | n | s |

  2   **3**

3. Parents also say that children spend too much time playing games and easily TGE DECDIDAT OT them.

| g | e | t | | a | d | d | i | c | t | e | d | | t | o |

  4   **5**

4. Many people say that it is healthy for kids to stay VTCEAI by doing other activities such as sports.

g	a	m	e	r	s

6

5. Playing video games can improve a person's vision, the ability to see things. It can also improve hand-eye INOTCROAINDO.

c	o	o	r	d	i	n	a	t	i	o	n

7

6. Good video games help children to think and learn. Many games teach players new information or make players solve UZLPZSE.

P	u	z	z	l	e	s

8 9

7. People like to learn with games because they are both HLGLACNGEIN and fun.

C	h	a	l	l	e	n	g	i	n	g

10

8. Many MRAGSE play games online or with friends.

a	c	t	i	v	e

11   12

9. In role-playing games, players play in a SYNATFA world where they can make up their own characters.

F	a	n	t	a	s	y

13   14

2 Figure out the saying. Copy the letters in the numbered squares from Exercise 1 to the squares below with the same numbers.

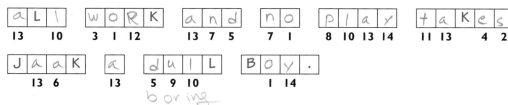

a	L	l
13	10	

w	O	R	K
3	1	12	

a	n	d
13	7	5

n	o
7	1

p	l	a	y
8	10	13	14

t	a	K	e	s
11	13		4	2

J	a	a	K
13	6		

a
13

d	u	l	L
5	9	10	

B	O	y	.
1	14		

boring

3 Discuss the saying with the class. What do you think it means?

EXPAND

1 CD 2 Read and listen to the conversation between two friends about a classmate's bad experience with computer games. Take turns reading the conversation with a partner.

A: Did you hear about that guy in our math class? The one who usually sits next to me?

B: No, what happened? I don't see him anymore.

A: I heard he started playing one of those online role-playing games, and now he plays it all the time. It **keeps him from** going to class. I heard he plays for several

(continued on next page)

hours every day. He hardly takes time to eat or sleep, and he rarely spends time with his friends anymore.

B: Are you serious? Why doesn't he **give it up**?

A: He can't stop. He's totally addicted to it.

B: That's **the problem with** those games. They're so good; it's hard to stop playing them. It's like you're living your life in the game. Before you know it, it becomes **a bad habit**.

A: Yeah, but can you really **blame** the game? I mean, no one **makes him** keep playing. He chooses to keep playing instead of doing other things.

B: That's true. That's why I really try to **limit** the time I spend on those games.

A: Yeah, me too.

2 *Choose the best synonym or definition for each underlined word or phrase.*

1. My busy work schedule <u>keeps me from</u> doing things with my friends.
   a. stops me from doing **b.** allows me to do

2. When did you <u>give up</u> playing video games?
   a. start **b.** stop

3. I don't see <u>the problem with</u> playing video games.
   a. what is difficult about **b.** what is bad about

4. I'm glad I didn't start smoking. It's <u>a bad habit</u>.
   a. something you do often that is not good for you **b.** something you don't like to do

5. My little sister always <u>blames</u> me when we have a fight.
   a. says I'm the cause of the problem **b.** hits me

6. My mother <u>makes me</u> finish my homework before playing video games or watching TV.
   a. asks me to **b.** tells me to

7. My mother <u>limits</u> the amount of money I can spend on new video games.
   a. counts **b.** controls

◖ CREATE

A game of Truth or Dare[1] is a good way to review vocabulary and learn more about your classmates.

1. Play in a small group. Use a die or pieces of paper numbered 1–6. The players take turns choosing a number.

2. After choosing a number, the player looks at the corresponding number in the chart and decides whether to "Tell the Truth" or "Take a Dare."

---

[1]**dare:** to challenge someone to do something that is difficult or embarrassing

Tell the Truth

Complete the task truthfully.

1. Name a thing that was very *challenging* for you to do. Were you successful in doing it? Describe what happened.

2. Name a *bad habit* that you have or had. Did you try to *give it up*? What happened?

3. Name a thing, such as a video or computer game, that you *got addicted to*. Describe it.

4. Name something you try to *limit* in your life and why you want to limit it.

5. Did you ever *blame* someone for something? Did anyone every blame you for something? If so, what happened?

6. Name something or someone in your life that *keeps you from doing* what you really want to do. Explain.

Take a Dare *tell someone to do something*

Complete the task with a word or phrase you choose from the vocabulary box.

1. Give the definition of the word / phrase.

2. Spell the word / phrase without looking at it.

3. Say another word / phrase that has a similar meaning.

4. Say a word / phrase that has the opposite meaning.

5. Use some of the letters in the word / phrase to spell a new word.

6. Translate the word / phrase into your native language.

Take a Dare: Vocabulary Box

Cross off the word after a player uses it. Each word can only be used once.

active	check out	gamer	solve
adventure	coordination	habit	use weapons
blame	explore	limit	violent ✓
challenging	fantasy	puzzle	

B GRAMMAR: Adverbs and Expressions of Frequency

1 *Read the sentences. Look at the underlined words. Then answer the questions on the next page.*

I <u>always</u> do my homework before I play games.

My brother <u>usually</u> plays video games after school.

My sister is <u>often</u> on the Internet.

a. What are the verbs? Circle them.

b. What question do the underlined words answer?

c. In which sentence does the underlined word appear *after* the verb? What's the verb?

d. In all three sentences, what tense are the verbs in? Why?

ADVERBS AND EXPRESSIONS OF FREQUENCY

1. Some adverbs of frequency are: *always* *usually* *often* *sometimes* *rarely* *never*	I **always** do my homework before I play video games.
2. Some expressions of frequency are: *every (day, week, month)* *twice (a week)* *once in a while* *several times (a year)* *three times (a month)*	My friend checks for new games online **every week**.
3. Use adverbs and expressions of frequency to tell how often someone does something.	I **sometimes** play video games after school. I check my e-mail **every day**.
4. The verbs used with adverbs and expressions of frequency are usually in the simple present tense.	My mother **usually** *plays* the Sims™. My dad *watches* the news on TV **every night**.
5. Adverbs of frequency come after the verb *be*. Adverbs of frequency usually come before other verbs. *Sometimes* can also come at the beginning of a sentence.	My sister *is* **often** on the Internet. My mother **sometimes** *worries* that I play video games too much. **Sometimes** my father plays video games with me.
6. Expressions of frequency usually come at the beginning or the end of the sentence.	My friend calls me **every day**. **Once in a while**, we go to the movies.
7. Use *How often* ...? in questions about frequency.	**How often** do you go to the movies?

2 Work with a partner. Take turns asking each other about the activities in the list below (or think of your own activities). When your partner answers "Yes," ask how often he or she does that activity. Ask each other six questions. Your answers must include an adverb or expression of frequency from the list. Write down your partner's answers.

Example

A: Do you ever play video games?
B: Yes, I do.
A: How often do you play them?
B: I play video games every day.

Activities	**Adverbs and Expressions of Frequency**
play video games	once a day / week / month / year
use the Internet	twice a day / week / month / year
watch TV	three times a day / week / month / year
listen to the radio	every day / night / week / month / Sunday
send e-mail	several times a week / month / year
send text messages	once in a while
call a friend on the phone	rarely
read the newspaper	never
read a book	
go to the movies	
play sports or do something active	

C SPEAKING

◀ PRONUNCIATION: Joining Words Together

CD 2
🔊 *Listen to the conversation. Listen to how the words join together.*

A: I think my brother is addicted to video games.
B: You can't get addicted to video games!
A: Yes, you can. It's easy.

When a word ends in a consonant and the next word begins with a vowel, the words join together quickly.

CD 2
11 *Listen to the short conversation. Notice how the pronoun I joins to the next word.*

A: I always read the newspaper. It's important.

B: I agree. It's better than watching the news on TV.

When the word after *I* starts with a vowel, the two words are joined together with /y/:

I ʸ always read the newspaper.

I ʸ agree.

1 **CD 2** **12** *Listen to the sentences and phrases and repeat them. Then practice saying the sentences with a partner. Join words together smoothly.*

1. It's easy.
2. He got addicted to video games.
3. several times a week
4. How often do you play?
5. almost always
6. three times a day
7. once in a while
8. action-adventure games
9. I don't agree.
10. twice a day
11. They're interesting.
12. almost every day
13. I agree with you.
14. I almost always come on time.
15. I often relax at home on the weekend.
16. I enjoy going out with friends.

2 **CD 2** **13** *Listen to the conversation and fill in the blanks.*

1. **A:** _____ _____ do you _____

   _____ to eat?

2. **B:** Several _____ _____ _____.

   How _____ you?

3. **A:** _____ _____. It's _____, and it's convenient.

4. **B:** _____ _____. But sometimes _____ like to _____.

5. **A:** You know how to cook? _____ _____ cooking dinner for me some _____?

6. **B:** Well, just _____ yourself _____! But yeah, that's OK. _____ _____ this weekend? Saturday?

7. **A:** Sounds great! You know, _____ _____ to chocolate.

8. **B:** _____ _____ I'm not a baker. How about _____ _____ _____?

3 *Work with a partner. Check your answers. Look at the conversation. Find words that end in a consonant and are followed by a vowel. Underline them. Then practice the conversation with a partner. Join words together and speak slowly and clearly.*

◀ **FUNCTION: Disagreeing Politely and Offering Different Opinions**

Sometimes people have different opinions about issues. When you do not agree with someone, you should disagree in a polite way. You can also give your own opinion about the issue. There are several ways to disagree politely with someone.

STATEMENT	DISAGREEING POLITELY	GIVING A DIFFERENT OPINION
I think video games are fun.	**Actually,** I think video games are boring. **But don't you think** it's better to do something active?	**That's true, but** I prefer to go out with my friends. **You have a point, but** some video games are too violent. **Maybe, but I think** spending time with friends is more fun. **I don't know. I think** video games are boring.

Work with a partner. Take turns giving your opinions and disagreeing with your partner about the statements below. Use the phrases for disagreeing politely and giving a different opinion.

Example

A: I think reading a book is less relaxing than watching TV.
B: You have a point, but reading makes you think.

1. Reading a book is less relaxing / more relaxing than watching TV.

2. Calling someone on the phone is easier / more difficult than sending an e-mail.

3. The Internet is / isn't a convenient way to get information.

4. Going to the movies is more exciting / less exciting than playing sports.

5. Dancing is / isn't a fun way to stay active.

6. Listening to the radio is / isn't a good way to hear new music.

◀ PRODUCTION: Debate

In this activity, you will **have a debate about video games**. In a debate, two teams discuss different sides of the same topic. The topic of your debate is "Are video games a good way or a bad way to spend your time?" One team is pro (for) video games and will argue that video games are a good way to spend your time; the other team is con (against) video games and will argue that video games are not a good way to spend your time. Try to use the vocabulary, grammar, pronunciation, and language for disagreeing politely that you learned in the unit.*

Work in two teams. If you have a large class, you may divide into small groups and have several debates. Follow the steps.

Step 1: Choose which team will be pro and which will be con. If the class divides into several groups, make sure there is an equal number of groups for each position.

Step 2: Work with your team or group to prepare for the debate:
• Plan your *arguments* (ideas that support your opinion). Write an outline.

Example

Your team's position: Games are a good way to spend your time.

Argument 1: Video games are fun because they are challenging.
• Think about the possible arguments that the other team or group may make. Plan your counter-arguments (points you can use against the other team's arguments).

*For Alternative Speaking Topics, see page 105.

Example

Other team's position: Games are not a good way to spend your time.

Possible argument: It's easy to get addicted to games.

Counter-argument: You need to limit the time you spend playing games and not play every day.

Step 3: Debate the topic with the other team or another group. The two teams or groups take turns presenting their arguments and counter-arguments. Make sure each member of your team or group presents at least one argument and counter-argument.

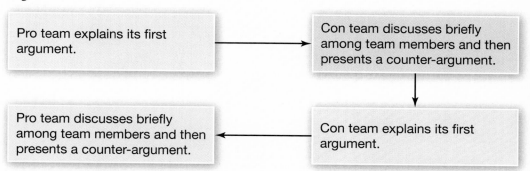

Repeat the process until both teams have presented all their arguments.

ALTERNATIVE SPEAKING TOPICS

Work in a small group. Discuss the questions.

1. Do you know anyone who is addicted to video games? How much time does he or she spend playing them?

2. Do you know any good video games? Why do you think they are good?

3. Do you think teachers should use video games in the classroom? Why or why not?

RESEARCH TOPICS, see page 191.

UNIT 7 Good-Mood Foods

1 FOCUS ON THE TOPIC

A PREDICT

Look at the pictures and discuss the questions with the class.

1. How do the people feel? Name the foods you see.

2. Which food do you think each person should eat? Why?

3. Read the title of the unit. What do you think it means?

107

B SHARE INFORMATION

1 *Why do you choose a particular food? Number the reasons in order of importance from* ***1*** *to* ***5***. *Number* ***1*** *is the most important and number* ***5*** *is the least important.*

_____ It tastes good.   _____ It's easy to cook.

_____ It's good for you.   _____ Everyone at my house likes it.

_____ It's cheap.

2 *Work in a small group. Explain why your number* ***1*** *reason is the most important to you.*

Example

A: I want food that's cheap because I have a big family.

B: I want food that's easy to cook because I'm a bad cook.

C BACKGROUND AND VOCABULARY

1 CD2 (14) *Read and listen to an e-mail about a stressful situation.*

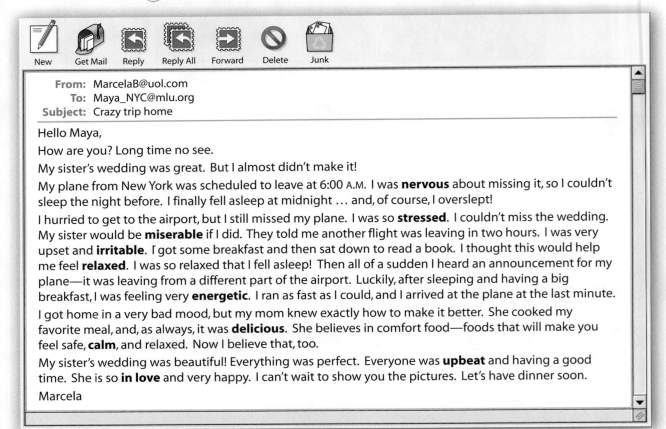

New   Get Mail   Reply   Reply All   Forward   Delete   Junk

From: MarcelaB@uol.com
To: Maya_NYC@mlu.org
Subject: Crazy trip home

Hello Maya,

How are you? Long time no see.

My sister's wedding was great. But I almost didn't make it!

My plane from New York was scheduled to leave at 6:00 A.M. I was **nervous** about missing it, so I couldn't sleep the night before. I finally fell asleep at midnight … and, of course, I overslept!

I hurried to get to the airport, but I still missed my plane. I was so **stressed**. I couldn't miss the wedding. My sister would be **miserable** if I did. They told me another flight was leaving in two hours. I was very upset and **irritable**. I got some breakfast and then sat down to read a book. I thought this would help me feel **relaxed**. I was so relaxed that I fell asleep! Then all of a sudden I heard an announcement for my plane—it was leaving from a different part of the airport. Luckily, after sleeping and having a big breakfast, I was feeling very **energetic**. I ran as fast as I could, and I arrived at the plane at the last minute.

I got home in a very bad mood, but my mom knew exactly how to make it better. She cooked my favorite meal, and, as always, it was **delicious**. She believes in comfort food—foods that will make you feel safe, **calm**, and relaxed. Now I believe that, too.

My sister's wedding was beautiful! Everything was perfect. Everyone was **upbeat** and having a good time. She is so **in love** and very happy. I can't wait to show you the pictures. Let's have dinner soon.

Marcela

2 Circle the best word or phrase to complete each definition.

1. When you are <u>nervous</u>, you are _____.
   a. worried or afraid   b. tired or sleepy

2. When you are <u>stressed</u>, you feel _____.
   a. worried about problems   b. quiet and safe

3. A <u>miserable</u> person is _____.
   a. very happy   b. very unhappy

4. When you are <u>irritable</u>, you are _____.
   a. easily annoyed   b. happy and cheerful

5. A <u>relaxed</u> person is _____.
   a. not worried or angry   b. upset

6. When you are <u>energetic</u>, you are _____.
   a. tired   b. active and full of energy

7. <u>Delicious</u> food _____.
   a. is good to eat   b. doesn't taste good

8. When you feel <u>calm</u>, you feel _____.
   a. quiet, not upset   b. in a hurry

9. An <u>upbeat</u> person is _____.
   a. sad and lonely   b. happy and cheerful

10. A person who is <u>in love</u> _____.
    a. feels love for someone   b. loves to do something

②FOCUS ON LISTENING

A LISTENING ONE: Street Talk

1 CD 2 🔵 *Listen to the excerpts from a radio talk show about daily life. Read the questions and discuss the answers with the class.*

1. Where do you think these people are? What are they doing?

2. How do you think these people feel?

2 *What do you think the people will talk about? Make predictions and write them below.*

_____

_____

LISTEN FOR MAIN IDEAS

CD 2 Now listen to the whole radio show called Street Talk. Then read each statement.
16 Write **T** (true) or **F** (false).

_____ **1.** Some doctors think that foods can change your moods.

_____ **2.** Some doctors say that eating certain foods will put you in a bad mood.

_____ **3.** Marty has foods that will help the people feel better.

LISTEN FOR DETAILS

CD 2 Listen to Street Talk again. Look at the chart and answer the questions.
17 (1) Check (✓) the correct mood for each person. (2) Check (✓) the foods that
Marty tells each person to eat. (3) Check (✓) the moods for each food.

	1. HOW DOES THE PERSON FEEL?	2. WHAT FOOD(S) CAN HELP THE PERSON FEEL BETTER?	3. HOW CAN THE FOOD(S) HELP THE PERSON FEEL?			
			Energetic	In Love	Relaxed	Upbeat
Larry	excited ❏ nervous ❏	chili peppers ❏ chocolate ❏	❏ ❏	❏ ❏	❏ ❏	❏ ❏
Dan	miserable ❏ stressed ❏	chocolate ❏ nuts ❏ wheat flour ❏	❏ ❏ ❏	❏ ❏ ❏	❏ ❏ ❏	❏ ❏ ❏
Barbara	stressed ❏ nervous ❏	turkey ❏ orange juice ❏ bread ❏	❏ ❏ ❏	❏ ❏ ❏	❏ ❏ ❏	❏ ❏ ❏

Now go back to Section 2A, Exercise 2 page 109. Were your predictions correct?

MAKE INFERENCES

Listen to two excerpts from the radio show. After listening to each excerpt, read the question and circle the correct answer. Discuss your answers with the class.

CD 2
🔘 18 **Excerpt One**

1. How does the man feel about tasting the soup?
   a. interested
   b. scared

2. How do you know?
   a. His voice rises.
   b. His voice sounds nervous.

3. How does the man feel after he tastes the soup?
   a. angry
   b. surprised

4. How do you know?
   a. His voice rises.
   b. His voice is soft / quiet.

CD 2
🔘 19 **Excerpt Two**

1. How does the woman feel when Marty offers her the food?
   a. scared
   b. angry

2. How do you know?
   a. Her voice sounds strong.
   b. Her voice sounds nervous.

3. How do you think she speaks to Marty?
   a. politely
   b. rudely

4. Why do you think so?
   a. She says, "I'm still waiting for the bus!"
   b. She says, "Are you crazy?"

EXPRESS OPINIONS

Discuss the questions with the class. Give your opinions.

1. What are your comfort foods—the ones that make you feel safe and calm? Are any of these foods from your childhood?

2. What are your favorite foods? Do you think they change your moods?

3. What other things do you do to change your moods? What do you usually do to feel relaxed, upbeat, or energetic?

LISTENING TWO: What's the Matter?

$\underset{\overset{\text{CD 2}}{\textbf{20}}}{}$ *Listen to four people: Kate, Derek, Jane, and Jeff. How does each one feel? Why do they feel that way? Write your answers in the chart.*

	KATE	DEREK	JANE	JEFF
1. How does the person feel?				
2. Why does he or she feel that way?				

C **INTEGRATE LISTENINGS ONE AND TWO**

◀ **STEP 1: Organize**

Work with a partner. Write the mood Kate, Derek, Jane, and Jeff are in. Then decide what food(s) each person should eat to feel better. Choose words from the box.

chili peppers	excited	miserable	oranges	turkey
chocolate	irritable	nervous	stressed out	wheat bread

	PERSON'S MOOD	FOOD(S) THE PERSON SHOULD EAT TO FEEL BETTER
Kate		
Derek		
Jane		
Jeff		

Discuss your answers with the class. Why did you choose that food? What else do you think the person should do to feel better?

Work with the same partner. Take turns. You will each discuss two people—Kate, Derek, Jane, or Jeff. Start by describing their moods (how they feel and why). Then tell which foods they should eat to feel better. Finally, describe their moods after they eat the food. How will they feel? Use the information from Step 1.

③ FOCUS ON SPEAKING

Ⓐ VOCABULARY

◖ REVIEW

1 Work with a partner. Each of the words and phrases in the box can be used with one of the verbs in the chart. Some words and phrases can be used with more than one verb. Complete the chart. Then think of two more words or phrases to add to each column.

chili peppers	excited	miserable	stressed out
delicious	in love	~~nervous~~	turkey
energetic	irritable	nuts	wheat flour

BE	FEEL	LOOK	MADE WITH	SMELL	TASTE
nervous	nervous	nervous			

2 Discuss the words in Exercise I with your class. Take turns making sentences using the words and the verbs from the chart.

Example

A: I'm so nervous about the party.

B: I feel nervous about cooking for a lot of people.

1 Read the flyer from a college cafeteria.

Don't let your mood get you down!
Eat happy and be happy!

Here are some suggestions to keep you in a happy mood all day:

- Eat five or six small meals a day. You'll have more energy.
- Always eat breakfast. Studies show it's the most important meal of the day.
- Eat a small snack before bed. It can help you relax and sleep well.

Sample menu:

 Breakfast

Hot cereal, like oatmeal cooked with milk and served with fruit jam served on whole wheat toast

 Snack

A bowl of rice seasoned with mint and served with iced tea

 Lunch

Tuna salad made with vegetables, served on lettuce

 Snack

A smoothie drink made with bananas, peaches, strawberries, and yogurt

 Dinner

Fish cooked in a light sauce, flavored with lemon and herbs, served with vegetables

 Snack

Crackers and fruit

Next time you are in a bad mood, eat something!

2 Fill in the chart on the next page with words from the box. Look back at the flyer to find which words go together. Words can be used multiple times.

cooked	in	on	seasoned	with
flavored	made	prepared	served	

cooked with

◖ CREATE

Work with a partner. Describe the pictures using the words from the box. Each student says two sentences about each picture.

Example

Picture 1
STUDENT A: The cook prepared some delicious chicken.
STUDENT B: It is served on rice with vegetables.

Picture 1

Verbs		Prepositions	Adjectives
be (is, are)	season	in	delicious
cook	serve	on	energetic
feel	smell	with	in love
flavor	taste		irritable
look			miserable
made			nervous
prepare			stressed out

Picture 2

Picture 3

1 *Read the sentences. Look at the underlined words. Then answer the questions.*

We'll have two <u>hamburgers</u>.

I would like some <u>soup</u>, too.

a. Is the word *hamburgers* singular or plural? Can you count hamburgers?

b. Is the word *soup* singular or plural? Can you count soup? What word comes before *soup* in the sentence?

COUNT AND NON-COUNT NOUNS		
1. **Count nouns** refer to people or things that can be counted. They can be singular or plural.	**Singular** one **customer** one **restaurant**	**Plural** two **customers** two **restaurants**
Use *a* or *an* before a singular count noun.	I ate **a sandwich** and **an orange**.	
To form the plural of a count noun, add **-s** or **-es**. You may use numbers with count nouns.	He ate **two sandwiches**, **three oranges**, and **five bananas**.	
2. **Non-count nouns** refer to things that cannot be counted. Do not put *a*, *an*, or a number before a non-count noun. Do not add *-s* or *-es* to a non-count noun because non-count nouns do not have a plural form.	I like **orange juice**. We love **fish**.	
Use a **quantity word** (*a glass of, a pound of,* etc.) to indicate the amount of a non-count noun.	Have **a glass of orange juice**. We need **a pound of fish**.	
3. Use *some* with plural count nouns and non-count nouns in affirmative statements.	I bought **some apples**. Have **some milk**.	
4. Use *any* with plural count nouns and non-count nouns in questions and negative statements.	A: Do we have **any vegetables**? B: No, we don't have **any vegetables**. A: Do we have **any soup**? B: No, we don't have **any soup**.	

2 *Work with a partner. Play a game of tic-tac-toe.*

Student A and Student B, take turns making sentences with the foods in the squares. If the food is a singular count noun, say *a* or *an* before it. If the food is a plural count noun or non-count noun, say **some**. If you make a correct sentence, put a marker on top of the food. The first student to get three markers in a row wins.

3 Work with a partner. Take turns asking about the food on the shopping list. Use the question and answers from the box.

Question	Answers
Do we need any . . . ?	Yes, we need . . . No, we don't need any . . .

Example

A: Do we need any rice?
B: Yes, we need some rice. Do we need any chili peppers?
A: No, we don't need any chili peppers.

Shopping List

rice
~~chili peppers~~
flour
bananas
milk
~~coffee~~
~~apples~~
bread
~~sugar~~
~~carrots~~
orange juice
~~soup~~

C SPEAKING

◀ PRONUNCIATION: Vowels: /ʊ/ and /uw/

/ʊ/ is the vowel sound in the word *good* /gʊd/.

/uw/ is the vowel sound in the word *mood* /muwd/.

good /ʊ/

m<u>oo</u>d /uw/

When you say /ʊ/, your lips are rounded a little and your tongue is relaxed.

/ʊ/ is a short sound.

When you say /uw/, your lips are tightly rounded, pushed forward, and your tongue is raised in the back.

/uw/ is a long sound.

1 🔘 CD2 21 *Listen and repeat the sentence.*

I read a good book about mood foods.

2 🔘 CD2 22 *Listen to the words. Do the underlined letters have the /ʊ/ vowel sound or the /uw/ vowel sound? Write the words in the chart under the correct vowel column. Compare your answers with a classmate's.*

1. s<u>oo</u>n	5. s<u>ou</u>p	9. w<u>ou</u>ld	13. j<u>ui</u>ce
2. l<u>oo</u>k	6. L<u>u</u>ke	10. c<u>oo</u>kies	14. b<u>oo</u>k
3. c<u>oo</u>l	7. t<u>oo</u>	11. n<u>ew</u>s	15. n<u>oo</u>n
4. c<u>oo</u>k	8. c<u>ou</u>ld	12. f<u>oo</u>d	16. fr<u>ui</u>t

GOOD /ʊ/	MOOD /uw/
	soon

3 🔘 CD2 23 *Listen again and repeat the words.*

4 CD 2 ⓟ Listen to each phrase or sentence. Are the underlined vowel sounds the same or different? Write **S** (same) or **D** (different).

_____ 1. a g<u>oo</u>d c<u>oo</u>k

_____ 2. fr<u>ui</u>t j<u>ui</u>ce

_____ 3. g<u>oo</u>d s<u>ou</u>p

_____ 4. L<u>oo</u>k at L<u>u</u>ke.

_____ 5. It's t<u>oo</u> s<u>oo</u>n.

_____ 6. g<u>oo</u>d n<u>ew</u>s

_____ 7. C<u>oo</u>k the fr<u>ui</u>t.

_____ 8. C<u>oo</u>l the s<u>ou</u>p.

5 Work with a partner. Student A, ask one of the questions. Student B, listen to the question, choose an answer, and read it aloud. Switch roles after item 3.

Example

A: What would you like to drink?

B: I'd like some fruit juice, please.

Student A

1. What would you like to drink?

2. Should I look at Robert?

3. Do you have good news?

4. What should I do with the fruit?

5. What do you think about my soup?

6. What time do you want to meet?

Student B

a. Mmm, you're a good cook.

b. I'd like some fruit juice, please.

c. No, look at Luke.

d. Yes. I found the book.

e. I could do it at noon.

f. Cook the fruit first.

◀ **FUNCTION: Making Suggestions**

When making a suggestion, you can use *could*, *might*, or *can*.

STATEMENT	MAKING A SUGGESTION	ACCEPTING	REFUSING
I feel stressed.	You **could** eat some soup with chili in it.	That sounds good. I think I will.	That doesn't sound like a good idea.
I feel a little sad.	You **might** want to try some fruit.	Yes, I think I will.	I don't think so.
I have a big test tomorrow; I really need to concentrate and study tonight.	You **can** eat a delicious fish dinner.	Good idea!	Maybe not, but thanks.

Walk around the room. Approach one student. Tell the student what is bothering you. The student will make a suggestion using the food in the list. Accept or refuse the suggestion. Talk to at least five students. Use the information in the chart to help you.

Example

STUDENT A: I am really tired.
STUDENT B: You could try some orange juice.
STUDENT A: OK. That sounds good.

If you need help concentrating, try	bananas beef cheese chicken	eggs fish milk oatmeal	oranges potatoes spinach turkey
If you are stressed, try	cottage cheese eggs	fish turkey	
If you want to feel calm or relaxed, try	chili peppers milk	oranges peanut butter on toast	spinach wheat
If you are sad, try	chocolate fruit	leafy vegetables	
If you are tired, try	carrots chicken eggs	fish nuts oatmeal	orange juice potatoes

◀ PRODUCTION: Small-Group Presentation

In this activity, you will **design and present a plan for a restaurant that serves good-mood foods.** Try to use the vocabulary, grammar, pronunciation, and language for making suggestions that you learned in the unit.*

Work in a group of three or four. Follow the steps on the next page.

---

*For Alternative Speaking Topics, see page 122.

Step 1: Design the restaurant.

- Give your restaurant a name.
- Design the look of the restaurant. How many tables are there? What is the lighting like? What kind of music do you play? Does your restaurant have a logo (a picture or symbol)? Draw the dining room of your restaurant on a large piece of paper.
- Decide where you want to locate the restaurant.

Step 2: Work on the menu. Suggest dishes your restaurant could serve.

- Decide on eight to ten items to put on the menu for the restaurant. You might only serve one meal—breakfast, lunch, or dinner—or all three meals.
- Write up your menu. You can include soups, sandwiches, salads, drinks, and desserts. Give the items attractive names, for example, "calming chili pepper soup, served with whole wheat bread."

Step 3: Present your restaurant to the class. Use the poster to show the restaurant design and menu. Describe each dish and how it improves your mood.

Listening Activity

Listen to the presentations and answer the questions.

1. Which is your favorite restaurant and why?
2. Which dishes would you like to try? Write down three to five dishes.

ALTERNATIVE SPEAKING TOPICS

Work in a small group. Discuss the questions.

1. If you found out that some of your favorite foods were not good for your moods, would you stop eating them? Would you be willing to make big changes in your diet to feel better? Why or why not?
2. Describe an ideal meal. Discuss the food, the person(s) you would eat with, the place, and so on. Why is this ideal for you?

RESEARCH TOPICS, see page 192.

UNIT 8 An Ice Place to Stay

1 FOCUS ON THE TOPIC

A PREDICT

Look at the photograph and discuss the questions with the class.

1. Where do you think this picture was taken?
2. What is the man doing there?
3. What is the man wearing? What season do you think it is?
4. Read the title of the unit. What do you think it means?

123

B SHARE INFORMATION

1 *Look at a list of things people think about when choosing a place to visit. What things are important to you? Check (✓)* **Very Important, Somewhat Important,** *or* **Not Important.**

	Very Important	Somewhat Important	Not Important
weather (what the weather's like)	○	○	○
location (how far it is from home)	○	○	○
language (what language the people speak)	○	○	○
cost (how expensive it is to visit)	○	○	○
activities (things to do)	○	○	○
sights (places to see)	○	○	○
lodging (places to stay)	○	○	○
people (friends and family to visit)	○	○	○

2 *Compare your answers in a group. Tell why each item is very important, somewhat important, or not important to you.*

3 *One way to get information for planning a vacation is to search on the Internet. What are some other ways to get information for planning a vacation?*

C BACKGROUND AND VOCABULARY

1 🔊 *Read and listen to an excerpt from a travel guide to Sweden.*

Sweden is a very large country in northern Europe. Every year (**1**) **tourists** come from all over the world to visit Sweden's cities, see the interesting sights, and enjoy the outdoors.

Tourists planning a trip to Sweden can choose different things to do. People who prefer big cities can visit Stockholm, Sweden's capital. Stockholm is a beautiful city of islands. In Stockholm, tourists can visit its many beautiful old castles and churches. They also can go shopping, enjoy the art, or see a movie or a play.

Tourists who enjoy the outdoors can find plenty to see and do in Sweden. Forests cover 50 percent

Museums . . .

of the land and are home to many wild animals, such as bears, elk, foxes, and reindeer. There are 96,000 lakes in Sweden, and in the north there is a long range of tall mountains. **(2) Adventurous** travelers will want to explore the beautiful **(3) wilderness** that Sweden has to offer.

Tourists must think about the weather when choosing the best time to visit Sweden. In the summer, the days are long and warm. The sun shines almost all day and night. There are many outdoor activities to enjoy, such as swimming, hiking, or just relaxing on the beach. Winter, on the other hand, is cold and dark. The temperatures often go below **(4) freezing**, and sometimes there are only a few hours of sunlight each day. The long hours of darkness give tourists a chance to see the northern lights, a beautiful show of color in the night sky. When the sun is up, visitors can enjoy cold-weather activities such as cross-country skiing, ice skating, snowshoeing, snowmobiling, and dogsledding.

There are also different kinds of lodging in Sweden. Travelers can stay at large **(5) hotels** with many **(6) guest rooms**, or they can choose to stay at small country **(7) inns**, where they may be treated to a home-cooked breakfast. Those who want to save money and enjoy nature can stay at campsites and sleep outdoors under the trees in a sleeping bag.

. . . art galleries, . . .

. . . and theaters.

Northern Lights

2 *Match the words on the left with the definitions on the right.*

_g_ 1. tourists

_____ 2. adventurous

_____ 3. wilderness

_____ 4. freezing

_____ 5. hotels

_____ 6. guest rooms

_____ 7. inns

a. buildings where people pay to stay for a short time

b. liking excitement and new and unusual things

c. the temperature at which water turns to ice; very cold

d. small buildings where people stay for a short time, usually in the countryside

e. a large area of land with no buildings or farms

f. rooms where visitors can sleep

g. people who travel for pleasure

3 *What are these people doing? Write the number of the picture next to the correct words.*

_____ cross-country skiing

_____ dogsledding

_____ snowmobiling

_____ snowshoeing

2 FOCUS ON LISTENING

A | LISTENING ONE: An Unusual Vacation

1 🔊 CD2 26 *Listen to the beginning of* An Unusual Vacation. *Read each question. Then circle the correct answer.*

1. What are you listening to?
   a. a TV commercial
   b. a telephone recording
   c. a radio show

2. What is it about?
   a. travel information about Sweden
   b. airplane flights to Sweden
   c. winter activities in Sweden

2 *Make predictions. Circle your answer.*

1. What will you hear more about?
   a. campsites in Sweden
   b. large hotels in Sweden
   c. a special hotel in Sweden

2. Will you hear a conversation or recorded information?
   a. a conversation with a travel agent
   b. recorded information

3. What do you think it will tell you? (*Circle more than one answer.*)
   a. the name of the hotel
   b. the location of the hotel
   c. the cost of the hotel
   d. how to get to the hotel
   e. things to do at the hotel
   f. things to do near the hotel

◖ LISTEN FOR MAIN IDEAS

🔊 CD2 27 *Listen to* An Unusual Vacation. *Then read each statement. Write* **T** *(true) or* **F** *(false). Correct the false statements.*

_____ 1. The Ice Hotel is open all year.

_____ 2. The Ice Hotel is made of ice and snow.

_____ 3. The guest rooms are warm at night.

_____ 4. The Ice Hotel is a popular place to stay.

_____ 5. There are only guest rooms at the Ice Hotel.

_____ 6. There are many activities to do near the Ice Hotel.

An Ice Place to Stay **127**

◀ LISTEN FOR DETAILS

c^D2 Listen to An Unusual Vacation *again.* Check (✓) all the things you can find in the
28 Ice Hotel and the things you can see or do near the Ice Hotel.

Things in the Ice Hotel
(*Check five items.*)

_____ **1.** beds

_____ **2.** sleeping bags

_____ **3.** bathrooms

_____ **4.** closets

_____ **5.** an art gallery

_____ **6.** a restaurant

_____ **7.** a theater

_____ **8.** a church

Things Near the Ice Hotel
(*Check six items.*)

_____ **1.** a shopping center

_____ **2.** a museum

_____ **3.** cross-country skiing

_____ **4.** snowshoeing

_____ **5.** dogsledding

_____ **6.** snowmobiling

_____ **7.** ice skating

_____ **8.** wilderness

Now go back to Section 2A, Exercise 2 on page 127. Were your predictions correct?

◀ MAKE INFERENCES

Listen to three excerpts from An Unusual Vacation. *After listening to each excerpt, read
the question and circle the correct answer. Discuss your answers with the class.*

c^D2
29 **Excerpt One**

1. Why does the man say, "Wait a minute"?
    a. He wants the woman to speak more slowly.
    b. He wants to talk about what the woman just said.

2. How does the man feel about the temperature in the rooms?
    a. He is glad it's warmer than the temperature outside.
    b. He is surprised that it is so cold.

c^D2
30 **Excerpt Two**

1. How does the man feel when he asks, "So people really stay there?"
    a. He is surprised.
    b. He is excited.

2. What does the man mean when he says, "I see"?
    a. He can imagine what the Ice Hotel looks like.
    b. He understands what the woman is saying.

Excerpt Three

1. What does the man think about the cost to stay at the Ice Hotel?
   a. He thinks it's too expensive.
   b. He doesn't think it's too expensive.

2. Why does the man say, "You're kidding me!"
   a. He thinks the woman is making a joke.
   b. He is surprised about what the woman said.

3. What does the woman think about the cost to stay at the Ice Hotel?
   a. She thinks it's too expensive.
   b. She doesn't think it's too expensive.

◖ **EXPRESS OPINIONS**

*Do a survey of your classmates. Stand up and walk around the class. Talk to five students. Ask each person if he or she would like to stay at the Ice Hotel. Write their names, answers (**yes**, **no**, or **maybe**), and reasons in the chart. When you finish, report the results to the class.*

WOULD YOU LIKE TO STAY AT THE ICE HOTEL?		
Name	**Answer**	**Reason**
Kae	No	It's too expensive.
1.		
2.		
3.		
4.		
5.		

1 *Look at the three vacations from a travel website. What place does each vacation describe? What do you know about these places?*

Vacation A	Vacation B	Vacation C

HIMALAYAN
MOUNTAIN ADVENTURE

Do you love nature and beautiful scenery? Do you enjoy hiking and camping? Then this is the trip for you!

Activities:

Go _____

_____

Enjoy _____

_____

Meet _____

_____

Lodging: _____

_____

Time of Year: _____

Weather: _____

_____

SOUTHERN CALIFORNIA VACATION

This travel package will take you to Hollywood and Disneyland, the happiest places on Earth!

Activities:

Visit _____

_____

Take a tour of _____

_____

Go _____

_____

Also visit _____

_____

Lodging: _____

_____

Time of Year: _____

_____

Weather: _____

_____

BALINESE
CULTURAL HOLIDAY

Travel to the Indonesian island of Bali for a relaxing and educational vacation.

Activities:

Relax _____

_____

Study _____

_____

Learn how to _____

_____

Lodging: _____

_____

Time of Year: _____

Weather: _____

_____

_____   _____   _____

2 CD2 **32** *Listen to the recorded information from the travel website* Vacations around the World. *It gives information about three different vacations. Write the number of the vacation under the correct web pages.*

3 CD2 **33** *Listen again to* Vacations around the World. *Then complete the information on the web pages.*

C INTEGRATE LISTENINGS ONE AND TWO

◀ STEP 1: Organize

You have heard about four different vacations. Fill in the chart with the information about the different vacations. Then compare your answers with a partner's.

VACATION	TIME OF YEAR	WEATHER	LODGING	ACTIVITIES
The Ice Hotel	winter			visit theater, church, go snowmobiling, dogsledding, cross-country skiing, snowshoeing
Himalayan Mountain Adventure				
Southern California Vacation				
Balinese Cultural Holiday				

◀ STEP 2: Synthesize

Work with a partner. Create a conversation between two friends. Use the information from Step 1 to talk about the four vacation destinations.

Example

A: Let's try warm weather and cultural activities.
B: OK. That is the Bali vacation. The main activities are . . .

③ FOCUS ON SPEAKING

A VOCABULARY

◖REVIEW

Read each group of four words. Circle the words that are similar to the first word in each line. Then compare your answers with a partner's. Explain why the words are similar. Explain why the other one doesn't fit.

1. **amusement park**   lodging   art gallery   museum

2. **hotel**   campsite   sleeping bag   inn

3. **guest**   tourist   traveler   travel agent

4. **take a tour**   relax on the beach   go sightseeing   go shopping

5. **go hiking**   go to the theater   go swimming   explore the wilderness

◖EXPAND

1   *Read the article from a student newspaper.*

Traveling on a Budget

It's almost spring break. Are you tired of studying? Are you ready to take a trip and **(1) get away from it all**, but you don't have a lot of money? Don't worry! It's possible to travel **(2) on a budget** and still **(3) have a great time**.

One great way to see the world **(4) on a shoestring** is to **(5) go backpacking**. Just put some clothes in a backpack and you're ready to go. To save money, you can travel by bus, train, boat, or even a bicycle. For inexpensive lodging, you can choose to stay in **(6) youth hostels**. In youth hostels you can share a room with other travelers for very little money. It's also a great way to meet other travelers from different places. Traveling with another person is also a great way to have fun and save money. It will cost you less if you share the expenses of transportation, lodging, and food with a friend.

If you like to see a new place and help others at the same time, you might want to take a volunteer vacation. On a volunteer vacation, you travel to another city or country and help the people in that area. For example, you might help park rangers save the plants and animals. Or you might help people build new homes. On a volunteer vacation you really **(7) get to know** the people and place you are visiting because you usually stay with a local family and live like they do. It's not your typical vacation, but it can be a great **(8) experience**.

2 *Write the number of each boldfaced word in the article next to its definition.*

_____ **a.** travel by carrying your belongings in a bag on your back

_____ **b.** inexpensive places to stay where guests can rent a bed and share a common bathroom, kitchen, and lounge

_____ **c.** enjoy yourself very much

_____ **d.** go away to a place where you can forget your problems, work, etc.

_____ **e.** with limited money to spend

_____ **f.** something that happens to you

_____ **g.** meet and learn about

_____ **h.** using very little money

◖ CREATE

Make a list of three activities you did or places you visited in the past. Then list three activities or places you would like to visit in the future. Use the information from the box or your own ideas. When you finish, work with a partner and take turns telling each other about your activities and places. Your partner should ask follow-up questions to get more information. Use other vocabulary from Review and Expand.

Activities		Places	
explore the wilderness	go swimming	amusement park	museum
go backpacking	relax on the beach	art gallery	theater
go hiking	take a tour	campsite	youth hostel
go sightseeing		hotel	

Example

A: Last year I visited a museum.
B: What museum did you visit?
A: The science museum.

A: In the future, I want to stay in a campsite and go hiking.
B: Where do you want to go?
A: I want to get away from it all and go to the mountains.

Activities I did / Places I visited

1. _____

2. _____

3. _____

Activities I want to do / Places I want to visit

1. _____

2. _____

3. _____

B GRAMMAR: *Can and Can't*

1 *Read the sentences. Look at the underlined words. Then answer the questions.*

What <u>can</u> you <u>do</u> at the Ice Hotel?

You <u>can look</u> at paintings in the art gallery.

You <u>can't go</u> swimming.

   a. What are the verbs in each sentence? In what form is the main verb?

   b. What does *can* mean? What does *can't* mean?

CAN AND CAN'T	
Can is a modal. Modals are words that come before main verbs. They change the meaning of the verbs in some way.	
1. Use *can* to talk about ability, things you are able to do.	I **can** ice skate. I took lessons last year.
Use *can't* to talk about inability.	My brother **can't** ski. He's never tried it.
2. Use *can* to talk about possibility, things that are possible.	You **can** stay at the Ice Hotel only in the winter.
Use *can't* to talk about things that are not possible.	You **can't** stay at the Ice Hotel in the summer because it isn't there.
3. *Can* and *can't* come before the main verb. The main verb is in the **base form**.	[base form] You **can** go ice skating in Sweden. I **can't** go on vacation right now.
4. Use *can* and *can't* in questions and short answers. Do not use a main verb in a short answer.	**A: Can** you swim? **B:** Yes, I **can**. **A: Can** Ellen ice skate? **B:** No, she **can't**.

2 *Work in a group of three. You want to find out your partners' abilities. Before you interview them, write their names in the chart on page 135. Then write five yes / no questions with* can. *Interview your partners and note their answers in the chart.*

Example

A: Can you dance?
B: Yes, I can.
C: No, I can't.

134 UNIT 8

YES / NO QUESTIONS	NAME	NAME
Can you dance?	Yes	No
1.		
2.		
3.		
4.		
5.		

Share your information with the class.

Example

Miguel can dance, but Hiroshi can't. OR Miguel can dance, and Hiroshi can dance, too.

3 *Work with a partner. Look at the ad for Quebec's Ice Hotel in Canada. Take turns making statements about what is possible to do at or near Quebec's Ice Hotel. Your partner will agree or disagree with you.*

Example

A: You can see ice sculptures at Quebec's Ice Hotel.
B: That's right. You can.
B: You can swim at Quebec's Ice Hotel.
A: No, you can't. There isn't any pool.

Come to Quebec's Ice Hotel!
Near Quebec City, Quebec, Canada

❋ Have your wedding, reunion, or birthday with us!

❋ See our ice sculptures
Watch a movie in the theater
Sit on ice furniture
Sleep on an ice bed

❋ Go cross-country skiing
Go snowmobiling

❋ Visit nearby Montgomery Falls Park
See the 83-meter (272-foot) waterfall
Dine at a fine restaurant

◀ **PRONUNCIATION:** *Can* and *Can't*

Can: In affirmative statements and questions, we don't stress *can*. It is pronounced /kən/ and sounds like the last syllable of *bacon* or *Mexican*. The vowel in *can* is short and unclear.

Can't: Stress the negative word *can't*. The vowel sound in *can't* is clear and long /kænt/.

Note that *can* in short answers is stressed. The vowel is clear and long /kæn/.

🔊 **34** *Listen to the examples.*

You can only go to the Ice Hotel in winter. You can't go in summer.

A: Can I go snowshoeing near the hotel?
B: Yes, you can.

1 🔊 **35** *Listen and repeat the phrases and sentences. Pronounce* **can** *as* /kən/. *Join* **can** *to the preceding word.*

1. Mr. Bay can—bacon: Mr. Bay can cook bacon.

2. Joe can—chicken: Joe can cook chicken.

3. Maxy can—Mexican: Maxy can cook Mexican food.

2 🔊 **36** *Listen to the conversation and repeat the lines.*

TRAVEL AGENT: You can ski near the Ice Hotel.
CUSTOMER: Can you shop?
TRAVEL AGENT: No, you can't shop.

3 🔊 **37** *Listen to the sentences. Are they affirmative (* **can** *) or negative (* **can't** *)? Check (✓) the correct column for each sentence.*

Affirmative	Negative		Affirmative	Negative
1. _____	_____	4. _____	_____
2. _____	_____	5. _____	_____
3. _____	_____	6. _____	_____

4 Listen again. Write the sentences on the lines. Compare them with a partner's.

1. _____
2. _____
3. _____
4. _____
5. _____
6. _____

5 Work with a partner. Take turns reading the sentences from Exercise 4. Stress **can't** by saying it louder or longer. Do not stress **can**.

◖ **FUNCTION: Expressing Likes and Dislikes**

There are different ways to express likes and dislikes.

EXPRESSING LIKES	EXPRESSING DISLIKES
How do you like traveling?	*How do you feel about cold weather?*
It's **great**!	I **can live without** it.
I **love** it.	I **don't like** it **very much**.
I **really like** it.	I **don't like** it.
I **like** it.	I **can't stand** it.
It's **OK**. / It's **all right**.	I **hate** it.
I **don't mind** it.	

Work in a small group. Take turns asking and answering the questions. Use the expressions from the chart in your answers.

1. How do you like traveling?
2. What do you think about cold weather?
3. How do you like flying in airplanes?
4. What do you think about sharing a room with other travelers?
5. How do you like relaxing on the beach?
6. What do you think about amusement parks?

◀ **PRODUCTION:** Small-Group Presentation

In this activity, you will *give a presentation at a "travel fair"* about your group's favorite vacation destination. Try to use the vocabulary, grammar, pronunciation, and language for expressing likes and dislikes that you learned in the unit.*

Work in a small group. Follow the steps.

Step 1: As a group, make a decision about which vacation destination you want to present at the travel fair. It can be any kind of vacation—adventurous, relaxing, exciting, educational, or on a shoestring. After you make a decision, answer the questions and fill in information about your place in the chart.

TOPICS	QUESTIONS	YOUR DESTINATION _____
Weather	What's the weather like in _____?	
Best time of year	What's the best time of the year to visit?	
Activities	What can you do there?	
Sights	What sights can you see there?	
Lodging	Where can you stay?	
Cost	Is it expensive to travel there? Can you travel on a budget?	
People	Who will enjoy this vacation? (adventurous travelers, students, older travelers, families, singles, couples)	

*For Alternative Speaking Topics, see page 139.

Step 2: Make a travel poster about your destination that includes as much of the information in the chart as possible. Draw pictures or get photos of your vacation place to include.

Step 3: As a group, present your travel poster to the class. Tell the class why they will really like your vacation idea. Answer questions from the "audience."

Example

A: We know you will like this adventure vacation to Machu Picchu.
B: OK. Could you tell me about the weather there?
A: Sure. The best months to visit are from June to October. The weather is warm then.
B: Oh, I love warm weather. Can I go hiking?
A: Yes. You can hike on several different trails.

Listening Activity

Listen to the presentations and write down your vote for the best vacation. Count up the class votes for the best vacation. Discuss why you like or don't like the class choice.

ALTERNATIVE SPEAKING TOPICS

Work in a small group. Discuss the questions.

1. What do you think is most important for a good vacation: relaxing and getting away from it all, being adventurous, or getting to know the place and people?

2. If you could visit any place in the world, where would you like to go? Why do you want to go there? Would you rather return to a familiar destination or explore a new one?

RESEARCH TOPICS, see page 192.

Staying Healthy

①FOCUS ON THE TOPIC

Ⓐ PREDICT

Look at the pictures and discuss the questions with the class.

1. What is the man doing in each picture? How does he feel?

2. Do you think the man is healthy or unhealthy? Why?

3. The unit is about staying healthy. Make a list of healthy and unhealthy activities that you think will be discussed in this unit.

B SHARE INFORMATION

Work in a small group. Complete the activities.

1. There are many factors (reasons) that can affect your health. You can control[1] some of these factors; you cannot control others. Look at the list of factors. Write them in two categories in the chart.

age	gender (being a man or a woman)	stress
diet (what you eat)	sleep	weight
exercise	smoking	work
family history	social influences (work, friends)	

FACTORS YOU CAN CONTROL	FACTORS YOU CANNOT CONTROL

2. Staying healthy often depends on how well you can balance[2] the activities in your life. Look at the graph on page 143. It shows three categories: Work / School, Self-Care, and Social Life[3]. Then read the list of activities below it. Work in a small group and write the activities in each of the categories.

---

[1]**control:** to make something or someone do what you want or work in a way you want

[2]**balance:** to give same amount of importance to

[3]**social life:** activities that relate to meeting people, developing relationships with them, and spending time with them

GOOD HEALTH: A BALANCE

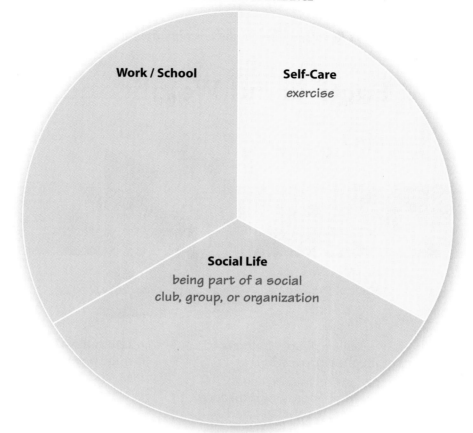

Work / School

Self-Care
exercise

Social Life
*being part of a social
club, group, or organization*

~~being a part of a social club, group,
or organization~~

changing bad habits (smoking,
   eating fattening foods)

earning money

~~exercise~~

going to events

healthy diet

learning new skills

preparing for a career

regular doctor visits

relaxation

sleep

spending time with family and friends

spiritual life

time away from work

---

3. In your group, discuss how much time you spend on these activities. How well
do you balance them? Do you spend more time on some than on others? How
can you live a healthier lifestyle?

1 🔊 *Read and listen to the brochure from a doctor's office about weight and health.*

Facts about Weight and Health

- More than one billion people in the world are overweight; they are too heavy.

- Overweight people have more health problems. They have more heart disease, high blood pressure,[1] diabetes,[2] and some kinds of cancer.[3] Remember, these are just some of the **side effects** of being overweight. Keep a healthy weight to help **prevent** these diseases.

- Many people who are overweight don't feel well; some feel **terrible**. They are often tired and have trouble breathing and sleeping.

- People try to lose weight in many ways:
  - Exercising
  - **Going on a diet** (eating foods with fewer **calories** and / or not eating certain foods that are **fattening** such as potato chips, pizza, or cheese)

- Using a weight-loss **remedy** (using pills, powders, drinks, and other products that help you to lose weight). Some remedies are **natural**, using **herbs**. Some are from your doctor, and some can be purchased at a store.
- Having weight-loss surgery (an operation to help lose weight)

- About 95 percent of people who lose weight will gain the weight back in one to five years.

- One recent study shows that having overweight friends may cause people to gain weight.

- According to the World Health Organization (WHO), the best way to lose weight and keep it off is to eat less and exercise more, so you can lose weight slowly.

For more information, talk to your doctor today.

---

[1] **high blood pressure:** when the pressure or force of the blood in your body is high
[2] **diabetes:** a disease of high blood sugar
[3] **cancer:** a serious illness which causes a growth to spread in the body

2 *Match the words and phrases on the left with the definitions on the right.*

___e___ **1.** calories

      2. fattening

      3. terrible

      4. herbs

      5. side effects

      6. natural

      7. go on a diet

      8. remedy

      9. prevent

a. very bad

b. stop something from happening

c. likely to increase your weight

d. eat less or eat certain foods to lose weight

e. energy in food that the body uses

f. unexpected results that a medicine has on your body

g. coming from nature; not man-made or artificial

h. plants used to make medicines or to flavor foods

i. something you can do or take to correct a health problem

2 FOCUS ON LISTENING

A LISTENING ONE: Thin-Fast

CD 2 *Some people use special products to stay healthy and keep a healthy weight. Listen*
40 *to a man talking about weight loss. Then read each question and circle the correct answer.*

1. What are you listening to?

  a. a radio commercial   **b.** a radio news show   **c.** a conversation in a doctor's office

2. What is Thin-Fast?

  a. a diet book   **b.** a weight-loss remedy   **c.** an exercise machine

3. What do you think you will hear about? (*Circle more than one answer.*)

  a. how to use Thin-Fast   **b.** how old it is   **c.** where it comes from

  d. what it's made of   **e.** how it makes you feel   **f.** how much it costs

CD 2
(41) *Listen to the whole commercial for Thin-Fast. Circle the best answer to complete each statement.*

1. Thin-Fast is a weight loss _____.
    a. pill
    b. drink
    c. powder

2. Mary Ann feels _____.
    a. overweight and unhappy
    b. thin and unhappy
    c. thin and happy

3. When using Thin-Fast, you _____.
    a. have to go on a diet
    b. have to exercise
    c. can eat fattening foods

4. The ingredients in Thin-Fast are _____.
    a. artificial
    b. natural
    c. unusual

5. Mary Ann thinks that Thin-Fast tastes _____.
    a. great
    b. terrible
    c. OK

◖ **LISTEN FOR DETAILS**

CD 2
(42) *Listen again. Then read each statement. Write **T** (true) or **F** (false). Correct the false statements. Then discuss your answers with the class.*

Thin-Fast . . .

_____ 1. helped Mary Ann lose 75 pounds.

_____ 2. is a product you drink once a day.

_____ 3. stops you from feeling hungry.

_____ 4. prevents your body from taking in calories.

_____ 5. has some side effects.

_____ 6. has ingredients that are 2,000 years old.

_____ **7.** makes you feel energetic.

_____ **8.** comes in two flavors.

_____ **9.** can be bought over the telephone.

Now go back to Section 2A, Question 3 on page 145. Were your predictions correct?

◖ MAKE INFERENCES

Listen to three excerpts from the commercial. Then decide whether Mary Ann would agree or disagree with each statement. Circle your answer.

CD 2
43 **Excerpt One**

"There's nothing better for weight loss than Thin-Fast."

Mary Ann would agree / disagree.

CD 2
44 **Excerpt Two**

"I don't mind exercising as a way to lose weight."

Mary Ann would agree / disagree.

CD 2
45 **Excerpt Three**

"Something people used for so many years must be good."

Mary Ann would agree / disagree.

Compare your answers with a classmate's. Explain your answers using details from the listening.

◖ EXPRESS OPINIONS

Read the questions. Discuss your answers with the class.

1. Mary Ann says she looks thin and feels healthy after losing weight. Do you think most people want to lose weight for their looks or for their health? Explain your opinion.

2. Americans spend more than $40 billion a year on weight-loss products and services. Why do you think products like Thin-Fast are so popular?

3. Many companies sell products that promise to make you healthy without exercising or eating well. Do you think these products work, or are they just a scam[1]? Explain your opinion.

4. "Bad habits are like a comfortable bed: easy to get into, but hard to get out of." What do you think this quote means?

5. What are some bad health habits? Which bad health habits are the hardest to change? Why?

---
[1]**scam:** a dishonest way to get money from someone

LISTENING TWO: Being Healthy Is Good for You!

CD 2
46
Listen to the conversation between a patient and a doctor. Complete the chart with the information you hear.

A HEALTHY LIFESTYLE MEANS ...	GIVE UP ...	WAYS TO BE PHYSICALLY ACTIVE
eating less		

C

INTEGRATE LISTENINGS ONE AND TWO

STEP 1: Organize

Fill in the information you heard about Thin-Fast and from the doctor for each of the categories listed in the chart.

	THIN-FAST	THE DOCTOR
Food and diet	eat anything	
Activity and exercise		
Amount of work to stay healthy		
How you'll feel		

STEP 2: Synthesize

Work with a partner. Act out a role play. Student A, you just heard about Thin-Fast and think it's an easy and great way to lose weight. Student B, you are a doctor who explains how you really lose weight. Talk about the four categories in the chart on page 148. Use the information from Step 1. Then switch roles.

Example

A: I just heard about a great weight-loss remedy. It's called Thin-Fast. It's so easy!
B: Really? Tell me about it.
A: Well, it's a drink. You can eat anything you want and you lose weight.

③ FOCUS ON SPEAKING

Ⓐ VOCABULARY

REVIEW

Complete the conversations with words or phrases from the box. Use the underlined words to help you. Then work with a partner. Practice reading the conversations aloud. Switch roles after item 4.

fattening foods	go on a diet	physically active	side effects
give up	healthy lifestyle	prevent	~~terrible~~

1. **A:** Cancer is a <u>very bad</u> disease. It kills nearly seven million people a year.

   B: I wish there was a cure for this _____terrible_____ illness.

2. **A:** Children don't <u>walk, ride bikes, or play outside</u> as much as they did in the past. That is one reason they are not as healthy now.

   B: Yes, kids today need to be more _____.

3. **A:** Scientists say that people who <u>stop smoking</u> will live longer. Each cigarette shortens life by 11 minutes!

   B: That is a great reason to _____ cigarettes.

4. **A:** Did you know that wearing a coat in cold weather won't <u>stop you</u> from getting sick?

   B: No. I thought dressing in warm clothes could _____ colds.

(continued on next page)

5. **A:** Some countries want to stop companies from advertising cookies, soda, and fast food to children. They say <u>eating these foods will make kids gain weight</u>.

   B: It's true that selling _____ to children can cause health problems.

6. **A:** One study showed that men who <u>did a lot of healthy things</u> were in less danger of having heart disease. They ate well, exercised, stayed thin, didn't smoke, and didn't drink too much.

   B: Wow! Those men had a very _____.

7. **A:** Some popular drugs can help you lose weight, but <u>they can also make you sick and cause heart disease</u>.

   B: Yeah. Weight-loss drugs can often have bad _____.

8. **A:** About 75 percent of women <u>eat less fattening foods</u> because they want to look better.

   B: Yes, but staying healthy is a better reason to _____.

◖ **EXPAND**

1 *Read the information from the website on sleep.*

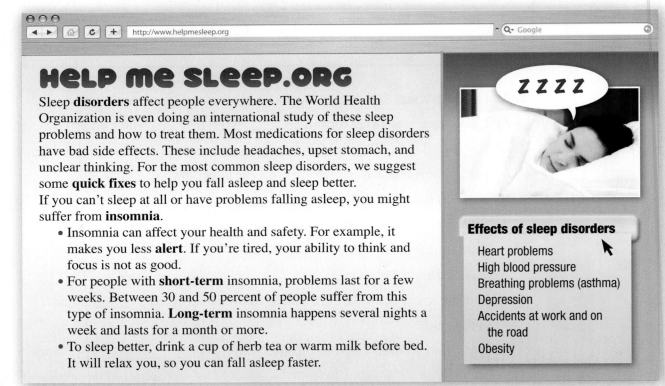

HELP ME SLEEP.ORG

Sleep **disorders** affect people everywhere. The World Health Organization is even doing an international study of these sleep problems and how to treat them. Most medications for sleep disorders have bad side effects. These include headaches, upset stomach, and unclear thinking. For the most common sleep disorders, we suggest some **quick fixes** to help you fall asleep and sleep better.

If you can't sleep at all or have problems falling asleep, you might suffer from **insomnia**.

- Insomnia can affect your health and safety. For example, it makes you less **alert**. If you're tired, your ability to think and focus is not as good.
- For people with **short-term** insomnia, problems last for a few weeks. Between 30 and 50 percent of people suffer from this type of insomnia. **Long-term** insomnia happens several nights a week and lasts for a month or more.
- To sleep better, drink a cup of herb tea or warm milk before bed. It will relax you, so you can fall asleep faster.

Effects of sleep disorders

Heart problems
High blood pressure
Breathing problems (asthma)
Depression
Accidents at work and on the road
Obesity

- Keep a piece of onion in a jar next to your bed. If you wake up during the night, sniff the onion to help you fall asleep again.

If you have a problem with **snoring**, or breathing loudly at night, try some of these remedies:
- Sleep on your side or stomach.
- Avoid drinking alcohol and smoking.
- Lose weight! **Obesity** is a main cause of snoring.

Some people stop breathing when they sleep. This may be a **risk factor** for serious health problems. **Get your priorities straight** and don't ignore this problem. Your health is important, so see your doctor immediately.

Risk factors

Get help

Search |

Contact Us   E-Mail Page   Print Page

2 *Match the words or phrases on the left with the definitions on the right.*

_____ **1.** disorder

_____ **2.** quick fix

_____ **3.** insomnia

_____ **4.** alert

_____ **5.** short-term

_____ **6.** long-term

_____ **7.** snoring

_____ **8.** obesity

_____ **9.** risk factor

_____ **10.** get your priorities straight

a. something that increases the chance of getting a disease

b. able to think quickly and clearly

c. for a short time

d. making a loud sound when you are sleeping

e. the problem of being very overweight

f. an illness or medical problem

g. think about the most important things first

h. inability to sleep

i. for a long time

j. a fast and easy solution to a problem

◖ **CREATE**

Work in a small group. Take turns asking and answering the questions. Use the boldfaced words and vocabulary from Review and Expand in your answers.

1. What are some things you can do to **prevent** health problems?

2. What do you do to be **physically active**? How can you have a **healthy lifestyle**?

3. Have you ever used a medicine that gave you **side effects**? Describe them.

4. What is one food you would never want to **give up**? Why?

5. What makes you feel **terrible**? What do you do to feel better?

6. What do you do when you have **insomnia**?

(continued on next page)

7. What are some **risk factors** of not getting enough sleep? Have any of these happened to you?

8. Do you know anyone with a medical **disorder**? What do they do for it?

B GRAMMAR: *Should, Ought to, and Have to*

1 *Read the sentences. Look at the underlined words. Then answer the questions.*

You <u>should</u> try Thin-Fast Diet Tea.

You <u>shouldn't</u> work so hard.

You <u>ought to</u> be more physically active.

You <u>have to</u> get enough sleep.

a. What are the verbs in each sentence?

b. In what form is the main verb in each sentence?

c. What does *should* mean? What does *shouldn't* mean?

d. What does *ought to* mean?

SHOULD, OUGHT TO, AND *HAVE TO*	
1. **Should**, **ought to**, and **have to** are modal verbs. Use **should** or **ought to** to give advice or to talk about what is right to do. Use **shouldn't** to talk about something that is not right to do. Use **have to** or **has to** to talk about something that is necessary. Use **don't have to** and **doesn't have to** to talk about something that is not necessary.	If you're sick, you **should** see a doctor. She isn't well. You **ought to** call her. You know you **shouldn't** drink. It's bad for you. I **have to** take medicine every day. She **has to** go on a diet. I **don't have to** go to the doctor today.
2. In affirmative and negative statements, **should**, **shouldn't**, **ought to**, and **have / has to** are followed by the base form of the verb. The modal verb and the main verb stay the same for each person. To form a negative with **have to**, use **don't** or **doesn't** before the modal. Use **have to** for each person. The main verb stays the same for each person.	You **should exercise**. She **ought to lose** weight. We **shouldn't work** so hard. I **have to give up** fattening foods. She **doesn't have to** sleep much. They **don't have to** eat less.
3. In questions, use **should** to ask for advice. Use **have to** to ask if something is necessary. **Ought to** is rarely used in questions or negatives.	**Should** I lose weight? Why **should** he see the doctor? Do I **have to** give up ice cream? Does he **have to** go to the doctor?

2 *Complete the conversation with the correct modal verbs. Then practice the conversation with a partner.*

A: Hi. How are you?

B: Oh, not great. I'm so tired. I was up all night studying, and now I have soccer practice.

A: Oh, that's too bad. Maybe you _____ go to
1.
practice today.

B: That's a good idea, but I _____ go because we have a big game
2.
tomorrow. Everyone needs me there.

A: I know! You _____ try one of those energy drinks. I hear they can
3.
really pick you up when you're tired.

B: Really? _____ I really
4.
have an energy drink before I exercise?

A: Why not? Energy drinks are full of natural ingredients and vitamins. And I heard that they can help you play better. A lot of athletes use them these days.

B: Well, I heard a news report about those energy drinks. It said that many of them are unhealthy. They have a lot of caffeine and sugar, and you really

_____ drink them before you exercise.
5.

A: Wow, I didn't know that. Then I think you _____ try the most
6.
natural remedy.

B: Really? What's that?

A: Sleep!

◖ PRONUNCIATION: Reductions

CD 2
47 *Listen to the underlined words in the conversation.*

A: How's your father? I heard he got out of the hospital last week.

B: Not very happy. His doctor says he <u>has to</u> quit smoking—no if's, and's, or but's. He <u>has to</u> stop.

A: Well, you know, I quit five years ago. He <u>ought to</u> start exercising when he quits. I did and I think it made quitting easier. Well, maybe not easier. But not so hard.

Have to, has to, and *ought to* are written as two words. Listen again. Do they sound like one word or two words?

HAVE TO, HAS TO, OUGHT TO	
Have to In speaking, *have to* is pronounced as one word, /hæftə/. The letter *v* is pronounced /f/. The vowel in *to* is usually pronounced /ə/	Do you have to /hæftə/ leave early? I have to /hæftə/ go now or I'll miss the last bus.
Has to In speaking, *has to* is pronounced as one word, /hæstə/. The vowel in *to* is usually pronounced /ə/.	He has to /hæstə/ quit smoking. She has to /hæstə/ learn to relax.
Ought to In speaking, *ought to* is pronounced as one word, /ɑtə/.* The vowel in *ought* sounds like the vowel in *father*. The vowel in *to* is usually pronounced /ə/. Native speakers of English often change the /t/ sound in *ought to* to a "fast D" sound: /ɑɒə/. *In some dialects of English, the vowel in *ought* is pronounced /ɔ/. This vowel is like the vowel in *saw*.	You ought to /ɑtə/ work less. He ought to /ɑtə/ start exercising.

1 *Listen to the conversation. Then practice the conversation with a partner.*
48 *Remember to use reductions.*

A: What's the matter? You look really tired.

B: I am. Sally—my wife—snored all night long. It was so loud that I couldn't sleep. Her snoring is getting worse and worse.

A: Well, you ought to use some ear plugs.

B: Then I won't hear my alarm clock. I don't know what to do, but I have to do something.

A: You just have to get some sleep, my friend. Maybe you should ask your wife to go to the doctor.

B: That's an idea. Or maybe she could try those new anti-snoring strips[1].

2 **49** *Listen to the sentences in columns 1 and 2 and fill in the blanks.*

1. Rosa, you look so
   _____*tired*_____. What's the
   _____?

2. Did you know that Jim just lost his
   _____? He's really
   _____.

3. My doctor said I really
   _____ lose weight,
   but I don't think I eat
   _____.

4. We need some _____.
   Life _____ be all
   work. We _____
   have some fun.

5. My roommate _____
   study tonight, so you can't
   _____ over.

6. My _____'s really
   slow. It's old, too. I think I
   _____ get a new
   one.

a. You _____ come to
   the gym with me. You'll lose
   _____ just by
   exercising.

b. That's OK. I _____
   study, too. Let's get
   _____ this
   weekend.

c. I _____ work late
   every night. I never get any sleep.

d. You _____ get a
   laptop. They're not
   _____, and they're
   very convenient.

e. You know I _____
   ask for a vacation now. I just
   started this job two weeks ago. I
   _____ work longer.

f. He _____ come to
   my office. My _____
   is looking for someone with his
   experience.

---

[1]**anti-snoring strips:** pieces of tape that are placed on the nose to keep the airways open during sleep

3 Work with a partner. Check your answers to Exercise 2 on page 155. Then match the sentences in columns 1 and 2 to make short conversations. Practice the conversations. Pronounce **have to, has to** and **ought to** carefully.

4 Work in a small group. Write a health or food problem that you have. Tell the group your problem. The other members of your group will give you advice.

Here's my problem:

_____

_____

_____

_____

◖ **FUNCTION: Expressing Concern, Giving and Receiving Advice**

When someone has a problem, it's polite to express concern and offer some advice.

EXPRESSING CONCERN	GIVING ADVICE	RECEIVING ADVICE
What's the matter? What's wrong? That's too bad. I'm sorry to hear that.	**Maybe you should** change your diet. **Why don't you** try to get some exercise? **I think you ought to** go to the doctor. **Have you tried** exercising?	That's a good idea. Thanks for the advice. I'll give it a try. Thanks anyway, but I'd rather . . .

1 Work with a partner. Look at the chart with health problems and ways to prevent them. Think of two more ways to prevent each problem and add them to the chart.

HEALTH PROBLEM	WAYS TO PREVENT IT
heart disease	have a healthy weight
diabetes	exercise at least 30 minutes a day
insomnia	read a book until you are tired
obesity	go on a diet
snoring	lose some weight

2 Walk around the classroom and talk to five other students. Practice expressing concern and giving advice.

Example

A: What's the matter?
B: My doctor says I have diabetes.
A: I'm sorry to hear that. Why don't you exercise at least 30 minutes a day?
B: Thanks for the advice. I'll give it a try.

◀ PRODUCTION: Public Service Announcement

Public service announcements (PSAs) are short (30-60 seconds) radio or television reports that send educational messages to the public. They give important information about specific issues such as health. In this activity, you will **prepare and present a PSA**. Try to use the vocabulary, grammar, pronunciation, and language for expressing concern and giving and receiving advice that you learned in the unit.*

Work in a group of three. Follow the steps.

cᴰ 2 **Step 1:** Listen to the following PSA about preventing a stroke[1]. Work as a class
50 to fill in the middle column of the chart.

	PREVENTING STROKES (PSA)	YOUR PSA
PSA Topic **Educational message**	preventing strokes	
Audience (children, adults, teenagers) **Tone** (serious, funny, sad)		
Sound Effects (sounds, noises, music)		
Advice in message		
Information at end of message		

Step 2: Write your own PSA on one of the topics from the unit.

- Decide on a topic and what you want your audience to do (stop smoking, get more sleep, lose weight, eat healthier food, be more active, etc.).

---

[1] **stroke:** a serious illness in which an artery (tube that carries blood) in the brain breaks or becomes blocked
*For Alternative Speaking Topics, see page 159.

- Decide on the audience, such as adults, teenagers, or college students.
- Decide what sound effects you will use.
- Discuss what advice you will give and what the announcer will say at the end. Fill in the last column of the chart on page 158 with your ideas.

Step 3: Present your PSA to the class or record your PSA at home and play it for the class.

Listening Activity

Choose your three favorite PSAs and fill in the chart. Discuss your choices with the class.

	TOPIC OF THE PSA	AUDIENCE	ADVICE	WHY DID YOU LIKE IT?
1.				
2.				
3.				

ALTERNATIVE SPEAKING TOPICS

1 *Work in a small group. Read the article and discuss the questions.*

In some cultures, obesity is thought to be beautiful and can show that a family is wealthy. Sometimes young girls are forced to eat to gain weight. But these girls can grow up to be obese and have health problems like high blood pressure and diabetes. Now some governments are trying to educate parents on health problems so these girls can grow up to be healthy women.

1. In this article, tradition and health are in conflict. What do you think about this?
2. Imagine your culture thinks something is beautiful, but it is bad for your health. Do you think you should have to change or not?

2 Work in a small group. Read the quotes about health. Explain each quote in your own words.

"Every human being is the author of his own health or disease."—Siddhartha Gautama

"It is health that is real wealth and not pieces of gold and silver."—Mahatma Gandhi

"To lengthen thy life, lessen thy meals."—Benjamin Franklin

"Leave all the afternoon for exercise and recreation, which are as necessary as reading. I will rather say more necessary because health is worth more than learning."—Thomas Jefferson

"To insure good health: eat lightly, breathe deeply, live moderately, cultivate cheerfulness, and maintain an interest in life."—William Londen

"If your dog is fat, you're not getting enough exercise."—Author Unknown

"Those who think they have not time for bodily exercise will sooner or later have to find time for illness."—Edward Stanley

---

RESEARCH TOPICS, see page 193.

RESEARCH TOPICS, see page 193.

UNIT 10

Endangered Languages

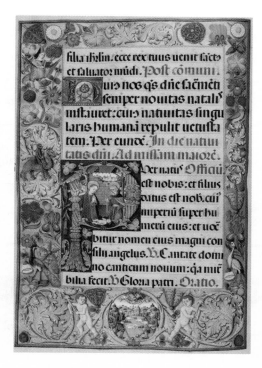

1 FOCUS ON THE TOPIC

A PREDICT

Look at the pictures and discuss the questions with the class.

1. What language are the people on the left speaking?

2. Do you recognize the language on the right? What is it? Do people speak it today?

3. Why do you think people stop speaking a language?

Work with a partner. Discuss the questions and write your partner's answers in the chart. Then share the answers with the class.

QUESTIONS	PARTNER'S ANSWERS
1. What is your native language (first language)?	
2. How many languages do you speak?	
3. Do you speak the same language as your parents?	
4. Do you speak the same language as your grandparents?	
5. What languages do you think the children in your family will learn? Do you want them to learn a different language?	
6. What is the official language (language used by the government) of your country?	

C BACKGROUND AND VOCABULARY

1 ^{C D 2} **51** Read and listen to an excerpt from a textbook about endangered languages.

LANGUAGE TODAY

Language Loss

There are more than 6,000 languages in the world today. Unfortunately, many of these languages are **endangered**. An endangered language is a language that few people are learning to speak. When an endangered language loses all of its speakers, it becomes **extinct**. Sometimes a language **disappears** when the language of a more **powerful** community **replaces** it. For example, this happened when English replaced many native languages in North America. Today, many Native Americans only speak English instead of their native language.

Many **linguists** study endangered languages and work to **preserve** them. A number of speakers of these languages also work hard to save them for future generations. In many communities, there are special programs that teach children their **native language**. These children grow up to be **bilingual**— they can speak the language of the more powerful community as well as their native language.

2 *Choose the best synonym or definition for each word or phrase.*

1. endangered
   - (a.) might die soon
   - b. already dead

2. extinct
   - a. no longer existing
   - b. very old

3. disappears
   - a. stops being useful
   - b. stops being used

4. powerful
   - a. strong
   - b. easy to learn

5. replaces
   - a. changes for something else
   - b. stops

6. linguists
   - a. people who speak the same language
   - b. people who study the science of language

7. preserve
   - a. save
   - b. lose

8. native language
   - a. a language only old people speak
   - b. a language that belongs to the place of one's birth

9. bilingual
   - a. speaking one language
   - b. speaking two languages

2 FOCUS ON LISTENING

A LISTENING ONE: Language Loss

🔊 CD 2
52
Listen to the beginning of a lecture on Language Loss. *Read and answer each question.*

1. Where is the speaker?
   a. in a class
   b. on TV
   c. on the radio

2. What is the topic?
   a. endangered languages
   b. endangered languages and cultures
   c. endangered and dead languages

3. What do you predict the speaker might talk about? (*List three possibilities.*)

   _____

   _____

   _____

LISTEN FOR MAIN IDEAS

🔊 CD 2
53
*Listen to the whole lecture. Then read each statement. Write **T** (true) or **F** (false).*

_____ 1. Linguists care about endangered languages because, when a language dies, a culture can die, too.

_____ 2. Languages become endangered when children don't go to school.

_____ 3. Linguists try to save endangered languages.

LISTEN FOR DETAILS

🔊 CD 2
54
Listen to the lecture again. Then circle the best answer to complete each statement.

1. By the year 2100, _____ of the world's languages could be extinct.
   a. 50 percent   **b.** 80 percent   **c.** 90 percent

2. The Manx people lost their native _____.
   a. culture   **b.** traditions   **c.** language

3. According to the speaker, _____ may be lost when a language disappears.
   a. books, schools, and teachers   **b.** culture, history, and knowledge   **c.** customs, communities, and way of life

4. Before 1987, it was _____ to teach Hawaiian in public schools.

    a. illegal   **b.** required   **c.** difficult

5. Today, more than _____ students are enrolled in Hawaiian language programs.

    a. 1,000   **b.** 2,000   **c.** 12,000

6. Once there were _____ Native American languages, but now many have become extinct.

    a. several   **b.** hundreds of   **c.** thousands of

7. In Greenland, students learn _____.

    a. Kalaallisut and Danish   **b.** only Danish   **c.** only Kalaallisut

8. Linguists help create _____ programs where people can study endangered languages.

    a. interesting   **b.** community   **c.** unusual

9. Linguists preserve languages by _____.

    a. recording them, studying them, and by writing story books   **b.** studying them, learning them, and writing history books   **c.** recording them, studying them, and writing grammar books

Now go back to Section 2A, Question 3 on page 164. How many of your predictions did the speaker discuss?

◖ MAKE INFERENCES

Listen to three excerpts from the lecture. After listening to each excerpt, answer the questions. Discuss your answers with the class.

CD 2
55 **Excerpt One**

    1. "My students come to class prepared."
        Would the professor agree or disagree?

        a. agree   **b.** disagree

    2. Why does the professor stress the word *some*?

        a. He thinks some of the students should listen more carefully.   **b.** He wants to stress that only some of the students did the reading.

CD 2
56 **Excerpt Two**

    1. "I was sure I had the right answer to the professor's question."
        Would Jessica agree or disagree?

        a. agree   **b.** disagree

(continued on next page)

2. How do you know?

   a. Her voice rises at the end of the sentence.

   b. Her voice falls at the end of the sentence.

 **Excerpt Three**

1. "Language is important for preserving culture." Would the professor agree or disagree?

   a. agree

   b. disagree

2. Why does the professor say, "moving on"?

   a. He is moving to another part of the classroom.

   b. He is changing the topic.

◖ **EXPRESS OPINIONS**

Work in a small group. Read the different opinions about language. Then say whether you agree or disagree with the opinions and explain why.

Language is a very important part of one's culture. That's why we should preserve languages.

to save

I think each country should have only one official language. People who live in the same country should speak the same language.

I think it's important for people to learn more than one language. That way they can understand different people and cultures.

controversial

sensitive
- feeling
effected

Listen to the class guest-speaker talk about her experience with her native language and culture. Then read each question and circle the correct answer.

1. Where does she live?
   a. New Zealand
   b. Greenland

2. What language did she learn in school?
   a. Maori
   b. English

3. What language did her grandparents speak?
   a. Maori
   b. English

4. How did she feel in her family?
   a. empty and different
   b. happy and excited

5. Where do her children learn Maori language and culture?
   a. in elementary school
   b. in language nests

6. What is a language nest?
   a. a pre-school
   b. a home school

7. What is / are the official language(s) of New Zealand now?
   a. English
   b. English and Maori

8. What are three Maori values that children learn?
   a. love, caring, and respect for elders
   b. hope, sharing, and family responsibilities

9. Who teaches the Maori adults their language and culture?
   a. linguists
   b. older Maoris

10. Where do they meet?
    a. in schools
    b. in neighborhood centers

Young Maori boys

◀ **STEP 1: Organize**

Work with a partner. In the chart, list the examples from Listening Two for each idea from Listening One.

REASONS FOR LANGUAGE LOSS	EXAMPLES FROM LISTENING TWO
1. Children don't learn the language in school.	Children only learned English, not Maori, in school.
2. Children stop learning the language and only old people speak it.	
3. Children don't learn the culture.	

WAYS TO SAVE LANGUAGES AND CULTURES	
1. Children learn the language and culture.	
2. The government makes the language official.	
3. Adults learn the language and culture.	

◀ **STEP 2: Synthesize**

Work with the same partner. Student A, you are the student asking questions; Student B, you are the professor giving examples. Begin by asking about the reasons for language loss, and then ask about ways to save languages and cultures. If the answer is not complete, ask a follow-up question, such as "Could you say more about that?" Then switch roles. Use the information from Step 1.

Example

A: Why are we losing so many languages?
B: One reason for language loss is because children don't learn their native language in school.
A: Could you say more about that?
B: Before, Maori children only learned English in school, so they couldn't speak Maori with their grandparents. Now, they learn Maori and English.

3 FOCUS ON SPEAKING

A VOCABULARY

REVIEW

Complete the conversations between a professor and a student with words from the box. Use the underlined words to help you. Then practice reading the conversations aloud with a partner. Switch roles after item 5.

bilingual	extinct	linguists	preserve
disappears	generation	official language	replace
~~endangered~~	language nests		

1. **A:** What do you call <u>a language that may die soon</u>?

   B: Is that a(n) _____*endangered*_____ language?

   A: That's right.

2. **A:** OK. What do you call a language that <u>no one speaks anymore</u>?

   B: That's a(n) _____ language.

3. **A:** So, who knows what happened when Native Americans <u>started speaking English instead of their native language</u>?

   B: They used English to _____ their native language.

4. **A:** What can happen when a language <u>goes away</u>?

   B: When a language _____, culture and history can be lost, too.

5. **A:** What happens when <u>parents</u> stop teaching their language to their <u>children</u>?

   B: The younger _____ won't continue to speak their language.

6. **A:** Why did people in New Zealand want to teach their children <u>to speak both Maori and English</u>?

   B: Because they wanted their children to be _____, right?

   A: That's right.

7. **A:** What else can people do to <u>save</u> languages?

   B: People can help to _____ languages by starting community programs where people learn their native language and culture.

(continued on next page)

8. A: Do you know what we call <u>pre-schools where children can learn their native language</u>?

B: Aren't those called _____?

A: Yes, that's it.

9. A: What can <u>people who study languages</u> do to save them?

B: _____ can study languages and write grammar books and dictionaries.

10. A: What about governments? What can they do to make sure a <u>language is spoken in government and schools</u>?

B: Can't they make a language a(n) _____?

A: Yes, that's right.

◀ **EXPAND**

1 _Read the article from a language preservation website._

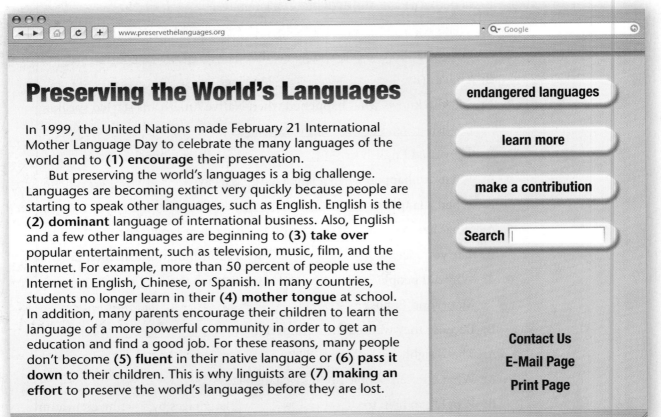

www.preservethelanguages.org

Preserving the World's Languages

In 1999, the United Nations made February 21 International Mother Language Day to celebrate the many languages of the world and to **(1) encourage** their preservation.

But preserving the world's languages is a big challenge. Languages are becoming extinct very quickly because people are starting to speak other languages, such as English. English is the **(2) dominant** language of international business. Also, English and a few other languages are beginning to **(3) take over** popular entertainment, such as television, music, film, and the Internet. For example, more than 50 percent of people use the Internet in English, Chinese, or Spanish. In many countries, students no longer learn in their **(4) mother tongue** at school. In addition, many parents encourage their children to learn the language of a more powerful community in order to get an education and find a good job. For these reasons, many people don't become **(5) fluent** in their native language or **(6) pass it down** to their children. This is why linguists are **(7) making an effort** to preserve the world's languages before they are lost.

endangered languages

learn more

make a contribution

Search

Contact Us

E-Mail Page

Print Page

2 *Write the number of each boldfaced word in the text next to its definition.*

_____ **a.** native language

_____ **b.** give something to younger people

_____ **c.** trying to do something

_____ **d.** gain control of

_____ **e.** having power over someone or something else

_____ **f.** to give hope and support to someone

_____ **g.** speaking or writing in an easy, smooth way

◖ CREATE

Work with a partner. Choose one of the situations below. Role-play the situation using the words in the box. Then switch roles. Practice both role plays, and then perform your best role play for the class.

bilingual	fluent	native language
dominant	generation	pass down
encourage	make an effort	preserve
endangered	mother tongue	take over
extinct		

Situation One

Student A, you are a parent. Your native language is endangered. You want your child to learn your native language at school, but the school only teaches English. You want the school to teach your native language.

Student B, you are the school's principal. You think all of the children should learn English at school because it is the dominant language in your community.

Situation Two

Student A, you are a parent. Your native language is endangered. You want your child to go to a community program to learn your native language, but your child does not want to go.

Student B, you are the child. You only want to learn English because all the children at your school speak it. You do not want to go to a community program.

1 *Read the conversation. Underline the verbs. Then answer the questions.*

> **A:** What will happen to the language?
> **B:** The language may disappear.
> **A:** Will children stop learning the language?
> **B:** Yes, they might.

1. What is the tense in each question? How do you know?

2. Look at each verb after *will* and *may* in the conversation. What is its form?

FUTURE WITH *WILL, MAY,* AND *MIGHT*	
1. Use **will** to . . . • talk about general facts about the future. • make predictions about the future that you are sure about.	Languages **will** die. Others **will** replace them. I **will** learn English in school.
2. Use **may** or **might** to . . . • express a possibility in the future. **May** and **might** have the same meaning.	Linguists predict 90 percent of languages **may** be extinct in 100 years. When a language dies, the culture **might** die, too.
3. To form statements with **will, may**, and **might** . . . • use **will, may**, or **might** plus the base form of the verb. • use the **contraction** of *will* (*'ll*) with pronouns. • do not use contractions in affirmative short answers.	Maori children **will be** bilingual when they leave the language nests. **They'll** speak both Maori and English. **She'll** be able to speak with her grandparents. **A:** Will they save their culture? **B:** Yes, they **will**.
4. To form a negative statement with **will** . . . • use **will not** or **won't** plus the base form of the verb. • notice the contraction. • use **won't** in negative short answers.	In Greenland, students are bilingual, so they **will not lose** their native language. They **won't lose** their native language. **A:** Will they lose their language? **B:** No, they **won't**.

5. To form a negative statement with *may* or *might* ... • use *may* or *might* plus *not*	Many Native American languages *may not* survive.

6. Use *will* to ask questions about the future.
 	
   • *yes / no* questions: use *will* + subject + base form of the verb
 	
   • *wh-* questions: begin the question with a *wh-* word
	Will we lose the language?
	
	When will we learn the language?

2 *Make groups of three. Read the questions. Make predictions using* **will, may,** *and* **might**. *Write the other students' answers and reasons for their predictions.*

QUESTIONS	NAME	NAME
1. Will your language disappear or will it be saved for future generations?		
2. Will the children in your family be bilingual?		
3. Will the children in your family speak the same language as your grandparents?		
4. Will you stop speaking your native language?		
5. Will language change because of the Internet?		
6. Will new languages appear?		

◀ PRONUNCIATION: Using Contractions with *Will*

When you speak, use the contraction *'ll* for *will* and **won't** for *will not*.

CD 2 59 *Listen to the examples.*

When my children start school, **they'll** learn English.

My children **won't** forget Maori, because **I'll** speak it at home.

Use *'ll* after pronouns: *I'll, you'll, she'll, he'll, we'll, they'll*.

When the word before *will* ends in a consonant, pronounce it /l/ and join it to the preceding word. The underlined words in the sentence below sound the same.

CD 2 59 *Listen to the example.*

<u>Nick'll</u> give me a <u>nickel</u>.

The contraction *'ll* is usually written only after pronouns. Even when the full form *will* is written, it is usually pronounced as a contraction.

WE WRITE: What will you do?
WE SAY: "Whattul" you do?

1 **CD 2 60** *Listen and repeat the sentences. Use contractions 'll and won't.*

1. When I have children, I'll make sure they speak Maori.

2. When they go to school, they'll study only English.

3. If you go to Greenland, you'll hear two languages.

4. If the language dies, the culture won't survive.

5. In 2100, there won't be as many languages as now.

6. In the future, many children won't speak the same languages as their grandparents.

2 Work with a partner. Student A, ask one of the questions. Student B, listen to the question, choose the correct answer and read it aloud. Use the contraction 'll when you can. Switch roles after item 4.

Student A

1. What will happen to many languages?

2. What will happen when the last native speaker dies?

3. How will children learn the native language of their country?

4. How will you preserve your native language?

5. Will you stop speaking your native language?

6. Why won't you speak your native language to your friends?

7. What will happen to a culture if a language dies?

Student B

a. No, I won't stop speaking my language.

b. They will disappear.

c. They will go to language schools and speak with other people.

d. Because my friends won't understand me.

e. The language will die.

f. The culture will disappear.

g. I will continue to use my native language.

◀ **FUNCTION:** Giving Reasons and Examples

Reasons and examples are used to explain general statements.

General Statement

PROFESSOR: Sometimes governments make it illegal to teach a native language in school.

Reason

This is because the government wants children to learn a different language.

Example

For example, before 1987 it was illegal to teach the Hawaiian language in Hawaii's public schools. The government wanted children to learn in English.

Here, the professor first makes a statement: He says that the teaching of language can be illegal. Then he explains the reason for this and gives a specific example of the Hawaiian language.

GIVING REASONS	GIVING EXAMPLES
This is because . . . The reason(s) for this is / are . . . One reason is . . .	For instance, . . . For example, . . . An example of this is . . .

*Student A, look at this page. Student B, go to page 187 and follow the instructions there. Student A, ask the questions below. Student B will answer based on the information given on his or her page. Ask follow-up questions with **why** to find out the reasons.*

Example

A: Why do languages become endangered?
B: Well, sometimes governments make it illegal to teach a language in school.
A: Why is that?
B: This is because the government wants children to learn the dominant language. For example, before 1987 it was illegal to teach the Hawaiian language in Hawaii's public schools. The government wanted children to learn in English.

Student A's Questions

1. What are people doing to save endangered languages?

2. What is happening to Native American languages?

Now switch roles. Student B asks you questions. Answer each question based on the information below. Make sure you use the phrases for giving reasons and examples.

Student A's Information

3. India doesn't have a single official language.

The government wants the different states to choose their own official languages. Telugu and Urdu are the official languages in the state of Andhra Pradesh.

4. Many native languages in Australia are nearly extinct.

Only a few adults speak them.
Only about 12 adults are fluent speakers of Wambaya, and no children are learning it.

◀ **PRODUCTION: Small-Group Discussion**

In this activity, you will *play the role of linguists discussing the future of some endangered languages and ways to preserve them*. Try to use the vocabulary, grammar, pronunciation, and language for giving reasons and examples that you learned in the unit.*

Work in a small group. Follow the steps.

Step 1: Look at the information about the endangered languages on page 178. Discuss the languages and why they are endangered.

- Predict the future of the language. Use *will*, *may*, and *might*. Give reasons and examples to support your ideas.
- Suggest things that you will do to save the language.

*For Alternative Speaking Topics, see page 179.

Example

ENDANGERED LANGUAGE:	*Mohawk*
NUMBER OF SPEAKERS:	About 3,000 fluent speakers
LOCATION:	North America: Ontario (Canada) and New York (United States)
DOMINANT LANGUAGE:	English
LANGUAGE PROGRAMS:	Some language programs in local schools and after school, but most children are not in these programs
	Adult programs have just started

A: Why is Mohawk endangered?

B: It's endangered because only about 3,000 people speak Mohawk. Most people speak English.

C: Do you think it will disappear soon?

B: I think it might because there aren't enough young people learning the language.

A: What will you do to preserve it?

B: There are some programs for adults to learn Mohawk but I'll start more programs.

C: I'll start language nests for young children.

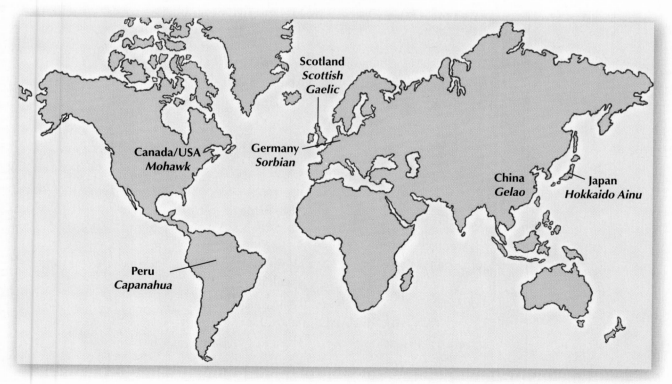

a. ENDANGERED LANGUAGE: *Sorbian*

NUMBER OF SPEAKERS: About 60,000, mostly adults

LOCATION: Germany

DOMINANT LANGUAGE: German

LANGUAGE PROGRAMS: Language instruction in some schools
Learned as a second language
Used in local government, radio, newspaper, and TV

b. ENDANGERED LANGUAGE: *Hokkaido Ainu*

NUMBER OF SPEAKERS: Possibly 40, almost all over age 30, very few fluent

LOCATION: Japan

DOMINANT LANGUAGE: Japanese

LANGUAGE PROGRAMS: Not taught in schools
Some community programs

c. ENDANGERED LANGUAGE: *Gelao*

NUMBER OF SPEAKERS: About 3,000, mostly older adults

LOCATION: southern China

DOMINANT LANGUAGE: Cantonese

LANGUAGE PROGRAMS: No language programs
Used in traditional religion

d. ENDANGERED LANGUAGE: *Scottish Gaelic*

NUMBER OF SPEAKERS: About 58,000

LOCATION: Scotland

DOMINANT LANGUAGE: English

LANGUAGE PROGRAMS: Bilingual programs in playgroups and school
Television programs in Gaelic
Efforts to make it official language with English

e. ENDANGERED LANGUAGE: *Capanahua*

NUMBER OF SPEAKERS: about 400, all bilingual adults; few children speak it

LOCATION: Peru

DOMINANT LANGUAGE: Spanish

LANGUAGE PROGRAMS: Used in two bilingual schools

Step 2: When you finish, report your group's ideas for preserving the languages to the class.

ALTERNATIVE SPEAKING TOPICS

Work in a small group. Discuss the questions.

1. Do you think people should do more to save endangered languages? Why or why not?

2. What do you think about learning English? How will it help you in the future?

3. Do you think learning English will threaten (hurt) your native language?

RESEARCH TOPICS, see page 194.

STUDENT ACTIVITIES

◀ **SHARE INFORMATION, Page 56**

Student A, study the photograph for <u>two</u> minutes; then close your book. Describe
what you saw to Student B.

Student B, study the photograph for <u>two</u> minutes; then close your book. Describe what you saw to Student A.

◀ **PRODUCTION, Page 71**

Student A

	JOHNNY MULDAR	LOUIS SILVER	DAN BLOCK
Current Age	45		
Home	New York City		
Work	1982–85, police officer		
Family	single		
Situation / Evidence	1985: Crime was committed. He was home at the time with his parents.		
Trial and Decision	1987: guilty Police did a bad job of collecting evidence.		
Sentence	life in prison		

Student B

	JOHNNY MULDAR	LOUIS SILVER	DAN BLOCK
Current Age		53	
Home		Montana	
Work		1980–1983, salesman	
Family		married with three children	
Situation / Evidence		1983: Eyewitness said she saw Louis.	
Trial and Decision		1984: guilty He had a bad lawyer.	
Sentence		40 years	

Student C

	JOHNNY MULDAR	LOUIS SILVER	DAN BLOCK
Current Age			67
Home			Chicago
Work			retired
Family			married, grandfather of 6
Situation / Evidence			1987: He gave a false confession.
Trial and Decision			1988: guilty Eyewitness did not tell the truth.
Sentence			life in prison

Exercise 2, Page 83

Student B, ask Student A about these classes. Write them in your schedule.

How to Make a Toast

Business Communication

Table Manners

	Monday	Tuesday	Wednesday	Thursday	Friday
6–7				**Telephone Etiquette** Learn: • to answer the phone politely • how to take a message • how to end a call	
7–8			**Social and Communication Skills** Learn: • how to greet someone • proper conversation topics • how to feel confident in any situation		
8–9		**Business Meals** Learn: • how to dress • where to sit • polite conversation topics • who pays the bill			

◀ **FUNCTION, Page 176**

Student B's Information

Student B, listen to Student A's questions. Answer each question based on the information below. Make sure you use the phrases for giving reasons and examples.

1. Linguists and other interested people have started organizations to help preserve native languages.

   They are concerned that many of the world's languages may disappear. The Foundation for Endangered Languages helps to study and preserve native languages.

2. Many Native American languages are endangered. More Native Americans are speaking only English.

   The Iroquoian languages like Onandaga and Mohawk, spoken in upstate New York and parts of Canada, have been slowly dying for more than 200 years.

Now switch roles.

Student B, ask the following questions. Student A will answer you based on the information given on his or her page. Ask follow-up questions with "why" to find out the reasons.

Student B's Questions

3. Does India have a single official language?

4. What is happening to the native languages in Australia?

RESEARCH TOPICS

UNIT 1: Offbeat Jobs

Would you like to find an offbeat job? Follow these steps:

Step 1: Work in small groups. Brainstorm some offbeat jobs and make a list. You can include jobs from the unit or other offbeat jobs that you know.

Step 2: Now, work alone. Choose one offbeat job you would like to have. Go to the library, look on the Internet, or interview someone who does the job to get information about it. Take notes. Your notes should include this information:

Job title:

_____

Workplace:

_____

Person has to be:

_____

Person has to like:

_____

Why the job is interesting:

_____

Step 3: Report your information to the class.

Listening Activity

Listen to your classmates' reports. Which job do you think is the most interesting?

UNIT 2: Building a Better Community

You're going to research the ways that your community has changed over the years. Follow these steps:

Step 1: Find someone who has lived in your community or a nearby community for many years. It could be an older relative, friend, or neighbor.

Step 2: Interview the person about the way your community is different now compared to many years ago. Use the following questions or think of your own.

    a. When did you first move to _____?

    b. Is _____ bigger or smaller now?

    c. How is the community designed now compared to back then?

     d. How is the housing different now?

     e. Are there any new businesses? Are there any businesses that closed?

     f. Is transportation different now? Do people walk more or less now?

     g. Do you think it is a better or a worse place to live now? Why do you think so?

  3. Report your findings to the class and compare your answers.

UNIT 3: A Penny Saved Is a Penny Earned

Before you buy something, especially something expensive, it's a good idea to do comparison shopping. When you comparison shop, you compare the different choices and then decide which is the best one to buy.

Practice comparison shopping for something you would like to buy. Follow these steps:

Step 1: Think of something you would like to buy, such as a camera, a television, or a jacket. Then go to a store and compare two different kinds. Or, go to two different stores to compare the prices. Answer the questions about your choice. Take notes and write the information in the chart below.

	ITEM 1	ITEM 2
How much does it cost?		
What does it look like?		
How well is it made?		
How big is it?		
Is it what you need?		
Do you want to buy it? Why or why not?		

Step 2: Report back to the class, telling which item you would like to buy and why.

(continued on next page)

Listening Activity

Listen to your classmates' reports and answer these questions.

1. Do you agree with the choice? Why or why not?

2. Which item would you like to buy?

UNIT 4: Innocent or Guilty?

Many countries now have DNA databases. You're going to research information and report about it to the class. Follow these steps:

Step 1: Go to the library or go on the Internet to find answers to these questions.

a. Does your country have a DNA database?

b. Is everyone's DNA in the database or just people who have committed a crime?

c. Does your country support Interpol's global database?

d. What are the pros and cons of an international database?

Step 2: Report back to the class with your findings.

UNIT 5: Etiquette

Work in groups of four. Do a survey like the one you heard about in Listening One. Do a door test, a paper drop, and a customer service test. Follow these steps:

Step 1: Go to a local café that has a variety of customers such as students and business people. Two students can do the study, and two can observe. Take turns.

Step 2: Fill in the chart with your results. Then compare your results to the results in Listening One. Are your results the same or different? Why do you think you got the results you did?

Step 3: Present your results to the class. Are your results similar to or different from other students'? Explain.

Describe the person (student, business person, etc.)	Door test: the person did / did not hold the door	Paper drop: the person did or did not help	Customer service: the person said / didn't say, "Can I help you?" "Thank you." etc.

UNIT 6: Who's Game for These Games?

You're going to research a video or computer game and report about it to the class. Follow these steps:

Step 1: Think of a video game you want to learn about. If you can't think of a game, look on the Internet or in an electronics store for a game that looks interesting to you.

Step 2: Go on the Internet and find information about the game:

    a. What's the name of the game?

    b. What kind of game is it?

    c. When was the game first made?

    d. How do you play the game?

    e. What are some good points about the game? What are some bad points?

    f. Why do you think you will like the game?

Step 3: Report your findings to the class.

Listening Activity

Listen to your classmates' reports and vote for the most interesting game.

UNIT 7: Good-Mood Foods

Interview someone you know about moods and foods. If the person knows about how foods can affect the mood, ask him or her the questions from the chart. Write the person's answers under "answers." If the person doesn't know, tell him or her what you have learned about moods and foods. Offer the person your suggestions and write them under "suggestions."

QUESTIONS	ANSWERS	SUGGESTIONS
1. How can food affect your mood?		
2. What do you eat when you are sad?		
3. What do you eat when you are relaxed?		
4. What do you eat when you are tired?		

Report information about your interview to the class.

UNIT 8: An Ice Place to Stay

The Ice Hotel is an unusual place to stay. You're going to research other unusual places to stay or visit. Work in pairs. Follow these steps:

Step 1: Go to a travel agency, a tourism office, or look on the Internet for information about an unusual place. Write a list of questions to get information about the topics listed in the card below.

Step 2: One of you asks the questions. The other one fills out the card. If you can, get some pictures of the place.

Name of unusual place:
Location:
Why it is unusual:
Weather:
Best time of year to visit:
Activities:
Sights:
Lodging:
Cost:

Step 3: Make a brochure with information about this unusual place.

Step 4: Show your brochure to the class and tell them about this amazing and unusual place. Show them any pictures you have.

Listening Activity

Listen to your classmates' presentations. Which place sounds the most interesting and unusual? Why?

UNIT 9: Staying Healthy

Are people's activities healthy or unhealthy? Find out by interviewing three people outside of class about their activities. Work with a partner. Follow these steps:

Step 1: Write at least five questions about healthy and unhealthy activities. Use the activities from the lists you made in Section 1B on page 142, and think of some more. Write the questions in the chart.

Example

How often do you exercise?

How often do you eat fattening foods?

Do you smoke?

QUESTIONS	NAME _____ (M / F) _____ AGE _____	NAME _____ (M / F) _____ AGE _____	NAME _____ (M / F) _____ AGE _____
1.			
2.			
3.			
4.			
5.			

(continued on next page)

Step 2: Now interview three people. One of you asks the questions. The other one writes down the answers.

Step 3: Report back to the class. Make sure you give the gender (male or female) and the age of each person you interviewed. Then discuss these questions.

- What are some healthy activities and some unhealthy activities of the people you interviewed?
- What health advice would you give to the people you interviewed?

Listening Activity

Listen to your classmates' reports. Do you think more people are healthy or unhealthy? Why? Who do you think are healthier, men or women?

UNIT 10: Endangered Languages

You're going to research an endangered language and culture. Follow these steps:

Step 1: Go to the library or use the Internet. Find out about an endangered culture and language (like the ones listed below).

| Breton | Cornish | Navajo | Chamorro | Sonsorolese |
| Trumai | Sare | Alagwa | Rangi | Ugong |

Use these questions to help you. Take notes.

a. What is the name of the endangered language?

b. Where is the language spoken?

c. How many people speak the language? How old are they?

d. Is anything being done to preserve the language?

e. Will this language survive?

Step 2: Report to the class. Tell them about this language and its future.

Listening Activity

Listen to your classmates' reports. Which languages are the most endangered?

GRAMMAR BOOK REFERENCES

NorthStar: Listening and Speaking Level 2, Third Edition	Focus on Grammar Level 2, Third Edition	Azar's Basic English Grammar, Third Edition
Unit 1 Descriptive Adjectives	**Unit 5** Descriptive Adjectives	**Chapter 1** Using *Be*: 1-6 **Chapter 6** Nouns and Pronouns: 6-2 **Chapter 14** Nouns and Modifiers: 14-1, 14-2
Unit 2 Demonstrative Adjectives *This / That / These / Those /* and *One*	**Unit 13** *This / That / These / Those;* Questions with *Or* **Chapter 14** *One / Ones / It*	**Chapter 2** Using *Be* and *Have*: 2-6, 2-7
Unit 3 Comparative Adjectives	**Unit 40** The Comparative	**Chapter 16** Making Comparisons: 16-3
Unit 4 Simple Past: *Yes / No* and *Wh-* Questions	**Unit 22** The Simple Past Tense: *Yes / No* and *Wh-* Questions	**Chapter 8** Expressing Past Time (1): 8-8 **Chapter 9** Expressing Past Time (2): 9-1, 9-2, 9-3
Unit 5 *Could* and *Would* in Polite Questions	**Unit 37** Requests, Desires, and Offers	**Chapter 13** Modals (2): 13-5
Unit 6 Adverbs and Expressions of Frequency	**Unit 26** The Simple Present and Present Progressive; Adverbs and Expressions of Frequency	**Chapter 3** Using the Simple Present: 3-2, 3-3, 3-4

(continued on next page)

NorthStar: Listening and Speaking Level 2, Third Edition	Focus on Grammar Level 2, Third Edition	Azar's Basic English Grammar, Third Edition
Unit 7 Count and Non-count Nouns	**Unit 25** Count and Non-count Nouns; Articles	**Chapter 7** Count and Non-count Nouns: 7-1, 7-2, 7-3
Unit 8 *Can* and *Can't*	**Unit 18** *Can / Could*	**Chapter 12** Modals (1): 12-1, 12-2, 12-3
Unit 9 *Should, Ought to,* and *Have to*	**Unit 38** Advice: *Should, Shouldn't, Ought to, Had better,* and *Had better not*	**Chapter 13** Modals (2): 13-1, 13-2
Unit 10 Future with *Will, May,* and *Might*	**Unit 31** *Will* for the Future; Future Time Markers **Unit 32** *May* or *Might* for Possibility	**Chapter 10** Expressing Future Time (1): 10-6, 10-7 **Chapter 11** Expressing Future Time (2): 11-1

AUDIOSCRIPT

UNIT 1: Offbeat Jobs

2A. LISTENING ONE: *What's My Job?*

Host: Good afternoon everybody, and welcome to *What's My Job?*—the game show about offbeat jobs. I'm your host, Wayne Wonderful. Today's first contestant is Rita, a secretary from Chicago, Illinois.

Rita: Hi, Wayne. I'm so happy to be here! Hi, Mom. Hi, Dad. Hi, Joe . . .

Host: OK, Rita. Let's get started. You're going to meet some people who will describe their jobs. Then you can ask three questions to guess each person's job. You can win $1,000 for each job you guess correctly. Are you ready? Let's welcome our first guest, Peter. OK, Peter, can you tell us a little about your job?

LISTEN FOR MAIN IDEAS

Host: Good afternoon everybody, and welcome to *What's My Job?*—the game show about offbeat jobs. I'm your host, Wayne Wonderful. Today's first contestant is Rita, a secretary from Chicago, Illinois.

Rita: Hi, Wayne. I'm so happy to be here! Hi, Mom. Hi, Dad. Hi, Joe . . .

Host: OK, Rita. Let's get started. You're going to meet some people who will describe their jobs. Then you can ask three questions to guess each person's job. You can win $1,000 for each job you guess correctly. Are you ready? Let's welcome our first guest, Peter. OK, Peter, can you tell us a little about your job?

Peter: Sure, Wayne. At my job, I work with food. My work is very interesting because I can enjoy good food and I can be creative.

Host: That does sound interesting. OK Rita, go ahead and ask your three questions.

Rita: Do you work in a restaurant?

Peter: No, I don't.

Rita: Hmm . . . do you work in a bakery?

Peter: No, I don't. I work in a factory.

Rita: A factory? Do you make food?

Peter: Yes, I help to make food.

Host: OK. That's three questions. Now Rita, can you guess Peter's job?

Rita: Hmm . . . are you a chef?

Peter: No, I'm not a chef.

Host: Ah, sorry Rita. So tell us, Peter. What do you do?

Peter: I'm an ice-cream taster.

Rita: An ice-cream taster?

Peter: That's right. I work in an ice-cream factory. I make sure the ice cream tastes good. I also think of interesting new flavors to make.

Host: Gee, sounds like a difficult job, Peter. You taste ice cream all day and you get paid for it!

Peter: Yes, that's right. I'm lucky to have such a great job.

Host: Good for you. So tell us Peter, is there anything difficult about your job?

Peter: Well . . . I guess so . . . For one thing, I can't eat all the ice cream. Otherwise, I'd get too full. I only taste a bit of ice cream and then I have to spit it out.

Host: I see. Is there anything else that's difficult?

Peter: Let me think. Well, I have to be very careful to take care of my taste buds. For example, I can't eat spicy or hot foods.

Host: Really?

Peter: Yes, and I don't drink alcohol or coffee . . . And I don't smoke, either. If I did those things, I might hurt my taste buds, and then I wouldn't be able to taste the ice cream very well.

Host: Wow! You do have to be careful.

Peter: Yes, I do. In fact, my taste buds are so important that they are covered by a one million-dollar insurance policy.

Host: One million dollars! You don't say!

Peter: That's right. You see, if I can't taste the ice cream, my company and I will lose a lot of money.

Host: Gee, you do have a very important job, Peter. So how did you get started as an ice-cream taster? Did you go to ice-cream tasting school?

Peter: Oh, no. My family has been in the ice-cream business for a long time. I've always wanted to work with ice cream, too.

Host: That's great, Peter. Thank you very much for being on the show, and keep up the good work! OK everybody, it's time for a commercial break. But, don't go away. We'll be right back with our next guest, on *What's My Job?*

LISTEN FOR DETAILS

(Repeat Listen for Main Ideas)

MAKE INFERENCES

Excerpt One

Peter: That's right. I work in an ice-cream factory. I make sure the ice cream tastes good. I also think of interesting new flavors to make.

Host: Gee, sounds like a difficult job, Peter. You taste ice cream all day and you get paid for it!

Peter: Yes, that's right. I'm lucky to have such a great job.

Excerpt Two

Peter: Yes, and I don't drink alcohol or coffee . . . And I don't smoke, either. If I did those things, I might hurt my taste buds, and then I wouldn't be able to taste the ice cream very well.

Host: Wow! You do have to be careful.

Excerpt Three

Host: Gee, you do have a very important job, Peter. So how did you get started as an ice-cream taster? Did you go to ice-cream tasting school?

Peter: Oh, no. My family has been in the ice-cream business for a long time. I've always wanted to work with ice cream, too.

2B. LISTENING TWO: *More Offbeat Jobs*

Job Counselor: Hello, I'm Nancy and I'll be your job counselor. I'm glad you've decided to come to this group; it's a good place to come to get ideas about new jobs or careers you might be interested in. It's helpful to listen to other people talk about their jobs when you're thinking of changing careers yourself. So, to begin, I'd like everyone to introduce themselves and tell us what your current job is and maybe why you are thinking of changing careers. I'll take some notes about what you say which, will help me suggest some possible new jobs. Hopefully we can find the right job for you! OK. Let's start with you.

Man: Hi, sure. My name is Mike and I'm a window washer.

Job Counselor: OK. Great. Why don't you tell me a little about your job?

Man: Well, I wash office building windows, so I go high up in the air in a basket to reach the windows.

Job Counselor: Sounds scary to me! Do you like it? And if so, why?

Man: Yeah, I really like my job because I enjoy being outdoors. I like to breathe the fresh air and look at the beautiful views of the city. It's really relaxing. I really don't think I could work indoors in an office or a store. And I earn a high salary . . . I make a lot of money. Window washing is a good job for me because I'm good with my hands. I don't like sitting in front of a computer all day. It was difficult for me to get started as a window washer. But I started my own business and I like that—working for myself—no boss, you know?

Job Counselor: OK . . . I'm just making some notes; like being outdoors, good with your hands, like being your own boss. OK. So why do you want a new job?

Man: Well, my job is pretty dangerous. I have to be very careful not to fall out of the basket, and I have to be careful not to drop things on people below. I just think I'd like something a little safer. Also, I enjoy it, you know, but it's a lot of work and can be very tiring. I go home at night and just want to sleep!

Job Counselor: Hmm . . . dangerous, wants something a little safer. OK. Great. Let's hear from the next person. Please introduce yourself and tell us a little bit about your job.

Woman: Hi, I'm Sarah and I'm a professional shopper. I go shopping for people who are busy and don't have time to shop. Basically, people give me a shopping list and some money, and I do the shopping for them.

Job Counselor: Well, if you like to shop, sounds like a great job.

Woman: It has its good and bad parts. What's good about it is that I do love to shop and I really like to work with people. I'm also very good with money. I always find clothes that are on sale—you know—cheap. But, well, the bad part is that my job isn't that easy. I'm on my feet a lot, so my work is tiring. And it wasn't easy to get started as a shopper. I worked for many years as a salesclerk in a department store. Then I started to meet people who needed a shopper. So, when I had enough customers, I quit my job at the department store and started my own business. Now, I'm my own boss but, well, I have to do everything myself and it's a lot of work. So, I wish I could just go to work, do my job, and then go home at night.

Job Counselor: Yeah, sometimes it's easier to work for someone else and let them have all the headaches! OK. Let's see . . . who's next? What's your name?

UNIT 2: Building a Better Community

2A. LISTENING ONE: *A New-Urbanist Community*

Host: New urbanist communities are designed to be different from typical suburbs. But how are they different? To find out, we sent Roy Martinez to a new suburban community called Kentville . . . Roy?

Roy: Thanks, Joanne. I'm here today in Kentville with the woman who designed this community, Elizabeth Jones. So, tell us, Elizabeth, why did you want to make a different kind of suburb? I mean, what's wrong with the typical suburb?

LISTEN FOR MAIN IDEAS

Host: New urbanist communities are designed to be different from typical suburbs. But how are they different? To find out, we sent Roy Martinez to a new suburban community called Kentville . . . Roy?

Roy: Thanks, Joanne. I'm here today in Kentville with the woman who designed this community, Elizabeth Jones. So, tell us, Elizabeth, why did you want to make a different kind of suburb? I mean, what's wrong with the typical suburb?

Elizabeth: Well, Roy, you know, most people in suburbs have to drive everywhere. People just spend too much time driving—sitting in their cars and stuck in traffic . . .

Roy: Well, that's certainly true, people do drive a lot. . . but what's wrong with that? Cars ARE convenient . . .

Elizabeth: Well . . . yeah, but sitting in a car isn't very healthy, and all those cars are bad for the environment.

Roy: Well, no doubt. That's true too, but people still need to get around. How is Kentville different?

Elizabeth: Well, I designed Kentville to be convenient for walking, instead of driving. To do that, I put the housing near the businesses and schools. So, as you can see, there are some houses here, but there's a school right down the street. And if you look over there, you can see there's a market on the corner where people can buy their food . . . and then right across the street there are some more stores and restaurants.

Roy: Uh-huh.

Elizabeth: Oh, and we also put some apartments and offices right above the businesses. So . . . basically, instead of driving, people in Kentville can just walk to where they need to go, kind of like a city neighborhood.

Roy: Hmmm . . . so people in Kentville WANT to walk more?

Elizabeth: Yep! I mean, believe it or not, they do! We put wide sidewalks down all of the streets to make walking easy AND we put the garages *behind* the houses instead of in the front. That way, the cars never cross the sidewalks, so it's safe to walk, too.

Roy: Huh . . . So how else is Kentville different?

Elizabeth: Well, I think Kentville is friendlier than most suburbs.

Roy: Really? How's that?

Elizabeth: Well, people in suburbs often don't even know their neighbors—people are isolated from each other. So, I wanted to make a community where people would get to know their neighbors, where they'd feel a sense of community.

Roy: Sounds like a good idea . . . but how can you do that?

Elizabeth: Good question. Well . . . If you look around, you'll see that the houses are built close together—so people live close to each other. And the houses are close to the street and they have front porches.

Roy: Oh yeah, I can see that . . . but how do front porches help?

Elizabeth: Well, with a front porch, people spend time in front of their house instead of inside, or in the backyard. They see their neighbors more and get to know them. And by getting out and walking down the street, people meet other neighbors and storekeepers and get to know them, too.

Roy: I see . . . so kind of like a small town.

Elizabeth: Right! And we also built lots of different kinds of housing—houses, condominiums, apartments—all near each other. I wanted a community where different kinds of people—families, single people, people in big houses and people in small apartments—could all live near each other.

Roy: OK. I see . . . but . . . don't you think most people want to be around people that are the same as them, not different?

Elizabeth: Huh. Well . . . maybe it's EASY to live around people that are the same, but I think a REAL community should have different kinds of people who can get to know each other and understand each other.

Roy: Interesting . . . Well, thanks for showing us around, Elizabeth. And good luck with your new community.

LISTEN FOR DETAILS

(Repeat Listen for Main Ideas)

MAKE INFERENCES

Excerpt One

Elizabeth: Well, Roy, you know, most people in suburbs have to drive everywhere. People just spend too much time driving—sitting in their cars and stuck in traffic . . .

Roy: Well, that's certainly true, people do drive a lot . . . but what's wrong with that? Cars ARE convenient . . .

Elizabeth: Umm . . . I guess that's true. But sitting in a car isn't very healthy, and all those cars are bad for the environment.

Excerpt Two

Elizabeth: So . . . basically, instead of driving, people in Kentville can just walk to where they need to go, kind of like a city neighborhood. . . .

Roy: Hmmm . . . so people in Kentville WANT to walk more?

Elizabeth: Yep! I mean, believe it or not, they do!

Excerpt Three

Elizabeth: I wanted a community where different kinds of people—families, single people, people in big houses and people in small apartments—could all live near each other.

Roy: OK. I see . . . but . . . don't you think most people want to be around people that are the same as them, not different?

2B.   LISTENING TWO: *Let's Hear from Our Listeners*

Host: Thanks for that report, Roy. Now, let's open up the phone lines to our listeners. So tell us . . . what do you think about this new community? Would you like to live in Kentville? OK, we have our first caller. Hello. You're on the air.

Caller 1: Hi. Well, I live in Kentville. And I think it's a great place to live . . . you really can walk everywhere IN Kentville . . . but one problem is there just isn't enough public transportation to get places OUTSIDE of Kentville. Most people still have to drive to work . . . Like me—I'm stuck in traffic right now!

Host: Oh . . . that's too bad. So public transportation is a problem. . . . Let's hear from another caller. Hello?

Caller 2: Hi. Well, I don't think I'd really like it in Kentville. I grew up in a small town—my family's lived there for years and years. I think in my hometown people really do feel a sense of community because we share a long history together. We really know each other . . . I don't think you can just make that happen in a new place.

Host: OK. Well, that's an interesting point. It takes time to build a sense of community. All right, we have time for one more caller . . . You're on the air . . .

Caller 3: Yes, hello. Well, I live in the city. So, I really like it here. It is pretty crowded and noisy, but it's an exciting place to live. I have a friend who lives in Kentville, and . . . it's a nice place to visit, but I wouldn't want to live there.

Host: Oh? And why is that?

Caller 3: Well, Kentville is so small, and there isn't much to do. And everything is so much the same. The houses and the buildings all look the same—and they all have rules that tell what color you can paint your house, and how you can decorate it. I think it's boring!

Host: Well, there you have it. A lot of people love Kentville, but not everyone is crazy about it. Until next week, this is Joanne Williams for *Newsline*. Goodnight.

3C.   SPEAKING

PRONUNCIATION: TH Sounds

Exercise 2

A: How far away is the theater? Should we drive?

B: No, everything's within walking distance in this town. Mom and Dad don't have to drive anywhere.

A: That's great. I don't like driving, either. But, you know, the houses are really close together. How do they feel about that?

B: They like it. You know, there's nothing wrong with being close to your neighbors.

UNIT 3: A Penny Saved Is a Penny Earned

2A.   LISTENING ONE: *A Barter Network*

Woman 1: Good morning, everyone. Let's get started . . . My name is Carol, and I'd like to welcome you to the City Barter Network. I'm glad you all could come to today's meeting. And I'm really happy to see so many people interested in joining our network. Now, there are a few things I'd like to do this morning.

LISTEN FOR MAIN IDEAS

Woman 1: Good morning, everyone. Let's get started . . . My name is Carol, and I'd like to welcome you to the City Barter Network. I'm glad you all could come to today's meeting. And I'm really happy to see so many people interested in joining our network. Now, there are a few things I'd like to do this morning. First, I want to tell you a little about bartering—what bartering is. Then I'll explain how you can barter in our network. Well, then, if you want to join, I'll sign you up as a member. Any questions? OK. Let's get started. First of all, does anyone know what bartering is?

Man 1: Bartering is trading stuff, right? Like, I trade my car for your computer, or something like that?

Woman 1: Well, that's one kind of bartering—trading one thing for another thing—but in our barter network, we only exchange services—things you can do for another person.

Man 1: Oh, I see.

Woman 1: Well, here's how it works. First, when you join the network, you sign your name on our member list and you list all of the services you can provide. Then every member gets a copy of the list or they can read it on our website.

Man 2: So, what kinds of services do members provide?

Woman 1: Well, most members provide services that a lot of people need like cooking, cleaning, or fixing things. But, ah . . . well, some people provide more unusual services like taking photographs, tutoring, or even giving music lessons.

Woman 2: Music lessons?! So, do you think I could get piano lessons? I've always wanted to learn how to play the piano.

Woman 1: Yeah, sure.

Woman 2: Wow! That's great!

Woman 1: It sure is! But remember that when you barter, you need to *provide* a service before you can *get* one . . . So that brings me to the next step, how to barter. After you become a member, another member can ask you to provide a service, to do something for them. For every hour of work you do for someone, you earn one Time Dollar.

Man 1: So, you can earn money?

Woman 1: Well, no, you can't. Time Dollars aren't *real* money. Basically, each Time Dollar just represents one hour of time that you spend providing a service. Later, you can spend your Time Dollars to get a service from someone else.

Man 1: So all the members earn one Time Dollar per hour, no matter what kind of work they do?

Woman 1: Yes. That's right. In our network, everyone's time is equal. No service is more valuable than another one. Oh, here, let me give you an example. A few weeks ago another member needed some help cleaning his house. I spent three hours cleaning his house, so I earned three Time Dollars. Then last week, my television broke and I needed to get it fixed. So I called another member who fixed it for me. He spent one hour fixing it, so I spent one Time Dollar. It was great! I saved money because I didn't need to pay anyone to fix it for me.

Man 1: I have a question . . . What if you don't know how to *do* anything? I mean I don't really have any skills . . .

Woman 2: Hmm . . . can you walk?

Man 1: Walk? Well, of course I can walk . . .

Woman 2: Then you can do dog-walking! I need someone to take my dog for a walk when I'm not home. Why don't *you* do it? . . .

Man 1: Well, I suppose I could . . .

Woman 1: Great! It looks like you're all ready to barter! But, let's get signed up first. Next, I'll pass out some forms . . .

LISTEN FOR DETAILS

(Repeat Listen for Main Ideas)

MAKE INFERENCES

Excerpt One

Man 1: Bartering is trading stuff, right? Like, I trade my car for your computer, or something like that?

Woman 1: Well, that's one kind of bartering—trading one thing for another thing—but in our barter network, we only exchange services—things you can do for another person.

Man 1: Oh, I see.

Excerpt Two

Woman 1: But, ah . . . well, some people provide more unusual services like taking photographs, tutoring, or even giving music lessons.

Woman 2: Music lessons?! So, do you think I could get piano lessons? I've always wanted to learn how to play the piano.

Woman 1: Yeah, sure.

Woman 2: Wow! That's great!

Excerpt Three

Man 1: I have a question . . . What if you don't' know how to *do* anything? I mean I don't really have any skills . . .

Woman 2: Hmm . . . can you walk?

Man 1: Walk? Well, of course I can walk . . .

2B.   LISTENING TWO: *The Compact*

Man: Hi there. I'm Mark.

Woman: Oh hi. I'm Natalie. It's nice to meet you.

Man: So, Natalie, tell me, why did you decide to join the City Barter Network?

Woman: Oh, well, I was looking for someone to fix my car. Luckily, I found somebody, and now I think I'm going to barter for piano lessons, too. How about you?

Man: Well, I'm looking for people to barter with because I belong to another group called the Compact.

Woman: The Compact? What's that?

Man: We're a group of people that made a compact—you know, like a promise . . . we promised not to buy anything new for a year.

Woman: No kidding! You aren't going to buy *anything* new for a whole year?

Man: Well . . . actually we *can* buy new necessities, things, you know, that you *need* for your health and safety . . . you know, like food and medicine.

Woman: That sounds hard. So why did you decide to do it?

Man: Well, we decided that we were spending too much money on *things*, you know . . . clothes, cars, electronics . . . we think most people just have too much stuff . . . stuff that they really don't need. We wanted to stop buying so much and learn to live with less.

Woman: I see . . . But you need to buy *some* things beside food and medicine . . . How do you get the other stuff you need?

Man: Well, we either borrow things from other people, or we buy things used at thrift stores . . . or we barter for the stuff we need.

Woman: Huh . . . so how's it going? Are you keeping your promise?

Man: Yeah . . . mostly . . . though sometimes we just *have* to buy something new when we can't borrow it or find it used . . . like, for instance, I needed to buy some new paint for my house. But that's it so far.

Woman: Wow! I bet you're saving a lot of money! How many members are in the Compact?

Man: It started out with only ten people but now there are thousands of members all over the world. . . . You should join us. You can do it online at our website.

Woman: Well . . . thanks, but I don't think I could do it. I like shopping too much—especially for new clothes! But hey, good luck!

3C. SPEAKING

PRONUNCIATION

Exercise 1

1. 13
2. 40
3. 50
4. 16
5. 70
6. 18
7. 19

Exercise 3

1. $7.50
2. $83.25
3. $319.40
4. $16.99
5. $1,500

UNIT 4: Innocent or Guilty?

2A. LISTENING ONE: *Roger's Story*

Roger: I recently got out of prison after 25 years. Now, you might not want to hear about that; maybe you think I should have been in prison. Maybe you think I did something wrong and I was guilty. But the truth of it is I didn't do anything wrong. I spent 25 long years in prison for something I didn't do. I was innocent; I didn't commit the crime they said I did. Can you imagine being in prison for 25 years when you're innocent? My name is Roger and I want to tell you my story.

LISTEN FOR MAIN IDEAS

Roger: I recently got out of prison after 25 years. Now, you might not want to hear about that; maybe you think I should have been in prison. Maybe you think I did something wrong and I was guilty. But the truth of it is I didn't do anything wrong. I spent 25 long years in prison for something I didn't do. I was innocent; I didn't commit the crime they said I did. Can you imagine being in prison for 25 years when you're innocent? My name is Roger and I want to tell you my story.

It all started in June 1980. I was living in Chicago and I had a good job. I just got married. One day, someone committed a crime. The victim told the police what the person looked like, even though it was dark out. The police showed the victim lots of pictures of people—about, I don't know, 200—and my picture was one of them. The victim looked at all those pictures and picked mine. She told the police I committed the crime and they just arrested me. Just like that. So one day I am working, trying to make a living, enjoying my life, and the next thing I know, I'm in prison.

In May 1981, there was a trial and I was convicted of the crime. They decided I did it even though I didn't. They sent me to prison for 13 to 40 years. You have to understand, I did not commit this crime. So you might be wondering how all this happened. How did the police arrest me and how did a lawyer show I was guilty? How does an innocent man go to prison?

Well, the lawyers had people who said they saw me do it; eyewitnesses, but they were wrong, or they didn't tell the truth. But the lawyers believed them. I told them where I was when the crime was committed; I was with my wife and some other family members. We went to a movie, came home, and watched some TV. I woke up in the morning and had breakfast, and left. My wife told the police that. So did other people in my family. But they said, of course, my family would say I was with them, and they didn't believe them. So I went to prison.

In 1992 after I had been in prison for 11 years, I heard about a new kind of test called DNA testing. It was being used to show people were innocent. I thought, "Maybe this could help me. Maybe this could prove I'm innocent", so I asked them to test my DNA. I knew I was innocent and if they tested my DNA, it would prove I didn't commit the crime. But to test DNA, you need some evidence that has DNA on it—something I touched. But they told me all the evidence was lost, so they couldn't test my DNA. I was so upset; no DNA, no test to show I was innocent.

Then, in 2000, I heard about an organization called The Innocence Project. It helps prove people are innocent using DNA testing. So I wrote a letter and asked for help.

The Innocence Project lawyers were able to get the police to find the evidence—it wasn't lost at all; it was exactly where it was supposed to be—and where it had been the whole time when the police said they couldn't find it. So they tested my DNA and it showed that the DNA from the crime scene was not mine; it proved I was innocent.

I was in prison for 25 years, because an eyewitness was wrong, the police didn't believe my family, and then the police couldn't—or wouldn't—find the evidence that showed I was innocent.

On July 1, 2006, I walked out of that courthouse a free man.

I'm one of more than 185 people that the Innocence Project has helped free. With this new kind of DNA testing, people who were convicted before can now show that they are innocent.

An awful lot happened in my life while I was in jail. I missed out on being with my family and I lost years of my life. I didn't see my children grow up. I had to learn how to live in the world all over again. Those 25 years . . . they're gone, and I'll never get them back.

LISTEN FOR DETAILS

(Repeat Listen for Main Ideas)

MAKE INFERENCES

Excerpt One

I told them where I was when the crime was committed; I was with my wife and some other family members. We went to a movie, came home, and watched some TV. I woke up in the morning and had breakfast, and left. My wife told the police that. So did other people in my family. But they said of course my family would say I was with them, and they didn't believe them. So I went to prison.

Excerpt Two

The Innocence Project lawyers were able to get the police to find the evidence—it wasn't lost at all; it was exactly where it was supposed to be—and where it had been the whole time when the police said they couldn't find it.

Excerpt Three

An awful lot happened in my life while I was in jail. I missed out on being with my family and I lost years of my life. I didn't see my children grow up. I had to learn how to live in the world all over again. Those 25 years . . . they're gone, and I'll never get them back.

2B. LISTENING TWO: *Why Do Innocent People go to Prison?*

Chris Meyers: Welcome back to "Morning Talk with Chris Meyers." We are talking to Laura Chang, a lawyer for the Innocence Project. Laura helped Roger Brooks, a man who spent 25 years in prison, prove that he was innocent. So, Laura, tell me, why do people go to prison for crimes they didn't commit? How's that possible?

Laura Chang: Well, Chris. There are several reasons why innocent people go to prison. But the number one reason is mistaken identity.

Chris Meyers: Hmm . . . mistaken identity? Is that when an eyewitness says he or she saw a person commit the crime, but in fact is wrong?

Laura Chang: Exactly. It happens because sometimes eyewitnesses don't remember correctly or they weren't able to *really* see well. They make a mistake because they have bad eyesight or maybe it was dark . . .

Chris Meyers: Aha . . . and they think they saw the person when in fact it was someone else?

Laura Chang: Exactly.

Chris Meyers: So, what are some other reasons why innocent people go to prison?

Laura Chang: Another reason is false confession—when people say they did something that they *didn't* in fact do.

Chris Meyers: Really? Why would people say that they committed a crime if they hadn't?

Laura Chang: Well . . . some people get scared . . . or don't understand what they're saying . . . or the police pressure them to say they're guilty . . . That happens.

Chris Meyers: So, you're saying police behavior might also be a reason why innocent people go to prison?

Laura Chang: Yes . . . and that makes me think of another problem I wanted to talk about. The police sometimes make mistakes, too. It's called police misconduct. In one case I worked on, the police actually destroyed some evidence—they stepped on it by accident, so the lawyers couldn't use it to prove the man was innocent.

Chris Meyers: Wow . . . interesting.

Laura Chang: Aha. But, the lawyer can also be the reason why an innocent person goes to prison.

Chris Meyers: Really? How come?

Laura Chang: Sometimes the lawyers just don't do a good job . . . they don't work hard enough to find the evidence to prove the person is innocent. Sometimes the first time a lawyer meets the accused person is the day they come to court together!

Chris Meyers: I see. So a bad lawyer can make things worse . . .

Laura Chang: Unfortunately, it does happen.

UNIT 5: Etiquette

2A. LISTENING ONE: *What Ever Happened to Manners?*

Host: Today our guest is Sarah Jones who recently did a survey of manners. I'll let her explain what she did. Welcome.

Sarah Jones: Thank you. It's great to be here.

Host: So, tell us what you did.

Sarah Jones: Well, it seems lately that many people are complaining that people are becoming very rude. So, we thought we'd try to find out if that's true. Basically, we did a survey of manners.

Host: Hm, I see. It seems that it'd be hard to test manners. How did you do it?

LISTEN FOR MAIN IDEAS

Host: Welcome back. In this part of the show, we're going to talk about manners. Many people feel that manners are disappearing—that people are becoming ruder. I think we'd all agree that it's easier to get along if we all follow some set of manners. But what is considered polite will be different depending on your culture. For example, in some countries, when you're invited to dinner at someone's home, you should arrive on time. If not, it's considered rude. But in other countries, when you're invited to someone's home for dinner, it's rude to arrive *on time*. You should instead arrive 30 minutes late! So, what's polite depends on where you are.

Today our guest is Sarah Jones who recently did a survey of manners. I'll let her explain what she did. Welcome.

Sarah Jones: Thank you. It's great to be here.

Host: So, tell us what you did.

Sarah Jones: Well, it seems lately that many people are complaining that people are becoming very rude. So, we thought we'd try to find out if that's true. Basically, we did a survey of manners.

Host: Hm, I see. It seems that it'd be hard to test manners. How did you do it?

Sarah Jones: Well, we sent two reporters to large cities all around the world—they went to 35 countries.

Host: Sounds like a great way to travel! So, who was part of your survey?

Sarah Jones: Well, we tested many different people: men, women, business people, high school students, police officers . . . anyone and everyone!

Host: And tell us about it.

Sarah Jones: Well, the reporters did three things. First, they did a "door test," second a "paper drop," and finally, they looked at customer service.

Host: Hm . . . Well, first off, what's a door test?

Sarah Jones: Well, we wanted to see if people would hold the door open for the reporters.

Host: Hm, that's a simple enough thing to do . . . OK, and then, a paper drop?

Sarah Jones: The reporters dropped a stack of papers, you know, like documents for work. We wanted to see if people would help pick them up. And finally, we looked at customer service. We wanted to see if people who work in stores were polite—you know, if they did courteous things like saying "hello," "thank you," things like that.

Host: So, what did you find?

Sarah Jones: OK . . . Well, in the most courteous city, 90 percent of the people passed the door test.

Host: Wow! You mean to say 90 percent of the people opened the door for the reporters?

Sarah Jones: Yes, that's correct.

Host: But opening the door for someone is an easy enough thing to do. You're opening the door anyway, right?

Sarah Jones: Well, true, but sometimes people aren't sure if they should hold the door open . . . I mean, how long should you hold the door for someone who is behind you but still far away?

Host: Yeah, sometimes it can be confusing; do I stand there holding the door waiting for someone who is walking towards me, or just go in and let them open the door for themselves? I can see that.

Sarah Jones: Right. So in general people held the door. But when we dropped our papers, only 55 percent helped pick them up.

Host: Huh, only 55 percent? That's not very good. But, I can imagine that sometimes you just can't help. I mean, what if your hands are full?

Sarah Jones: Yes, but one woman had two cups of coffee on a tray and her keys and wallet in the other hand. She put everything in one hand and helped! The reporter wanted to help *her!*

Host: Did the reporter ask why she wanted to help?

Sarah Jones: Well, she said, "I was standing there—of course I would help!"

Host: Huh, interesting. OK, now, what about customer service?

Sarah Jones: So, we tested people in a coffee shop; the same one in every city. And 19 out of 20 people said "thank you."

Host: So did they just do it because they're being paid?

Sarah Jones: Well, they *are* trained to be courteous. But others said they do it because it shows respect.

Host: You know, what I'm curious about is *why* did people say they were courteous?

Sarah Jones: That's a good question. This is where it gets interesting. Some said they were raised to be courteous. They said it was something they were taught when they were young. And other people said they do what they want other people to do for them.

Host: So it's what we learn and how we want other people to treat us. OK, so now, we've been waiting . . . of the 35 cities you studied all over the world, which city won?

Sarah Jones: Well . . . You're not going to believe this . . . It was New York City!

Host: You're kidding! That's certainly not what New York is known for. I'm so surprised!

Sarah Jones: We were too, but New York won!

Host: I would definitely never guess that! Wow!

LISTEN FOR DETAILS

(Repeat Listen for Main Ideas)

MAKE INFERENCES

Excerpt One

Sarah Jones: So in general people held the door. But when we dropped our papers, only 55 percent helped pick them up.

Host: Huh, only 55 percent? That's not very good. But, I can imagine that sometimes you just can't help. I mean what if your hands are full?

Sarah Jones: Yes, but one woman had two cups of coffee on a tray and her keys and wallet in the other hand. She put everything in one hand and helped! The reporter wanted to help *her!*

Excerpt Two

Sarah Jones: So, we tested people in a coffee shop; the same one in every city. And 19 out of 20 people said "thank you."

Host: So did they do it just because they're being paid?

Sarah Jones: Well, they *are* trained to be courteous. But others said they do it because it shows respect.

LISTENING TWO: *Our Listeners Respond— Why Is There a Lack of Manners?*

Host: Now is the time for listeners to call in and tell *us* what *they* think. We've just heard about an interesting survey of manners. So the question for our listeners is, why do you think there's a lack of manners? Caller one, you're on.

Caller 1: Hi. Well, I learned how to behave at home . . . from my parents. I think that's where a lot of people learn manners. But nowadays, parents are too busy; some moms or dads are raising children alone or have two jobs and just aren't home much. So there's less family time and that's where you learn manners—from your family, at home.

Host: Huh. That makes sense. So if more parents spend more time with their kids, we'll live in a more courteous world. Well, let's see what other callers have to say. Who's next?

Caller 2: Well, I live in a large city and one thing I notice is there are people living here from all over the world. When I walk down the street, I hear people speaking three or four different languages.

Host: So it's because we don't all speak the same language? That's why people are rude?

Caller 2: No, not that. Manners are cultural, right?

Host: Right. Sure.

Caller 2: And what's polite in one culture might not be polite in another. So when many people live together, sometimes it's hard to know what's right. It gets confusing.

Host: Hm . . . I can see why that could be true. OK. Let's take one more call.

Caller 3: Why are people rude? Technology. I think it's because of cell phones, text messaging, and the Internet.

Host: Well you certainly have a strong opinion!

Caller 3: Look, everywhere you go you see people talking on cell phones or text messaging; they're having a conversation with someone who isn't even there!

Host: Well, yeah. But cell phones and text messaging *are* very convenient.

Caller 3: Sure, but people have forgotten how to talk with someone face to face. Also, people expect an immediate response and they don't see a need to be courteous; they just write short messages. They forget to say things like, "how are you" and "thank you."

Host: Well, I like getting a fast response. Sometimes it's nice to *not* have a long conversation.

Caller 3: Look, I have a cell phone and I use text messages and I think they are useful. But I think people use them too much. Technology has made us more separate; we spend less time with people and more time on the phone.

Host: Well, we're out of time but to wrap up: we need more family time, a better understanding of our different cultures, and more face-to-face time . . . certainly some things to think about! That's all for now, until next week.

UNIT 6: Who's Game for These Games?

2A. LISTENING ONE: *Entertainment for All*

News Anchor: And now for some local news. Reporter Michelle Singh is down at the convention center where there's a gaming expo happening this weekend. Michelle?

Michelle: Hi Brad. We're having a lot of fun down here at the electronic games expo. This is a big event. Electronic game companies are showing all their latest games to the public. There are also gaming competitions and a video game rock concert. We're here talking to some people . . . so what do you think of the expo?

LISTEN FOR MAIN IDEAS

News Anchor: And now for some local news. Reporter Michelle Singh is down at the convention center where there's a gaming expo happening this weekend. Michelle?

Michelle: Hi Brad. We're having a lot of fun down here at the electronic games expo. This is a big event. Electronic game companies are showing all their latest games to the public. There are also gaming competitions and a video game rock concert. We're here talking to some people . . . so what do you think of the expo?

Man: Oh, I think it's great. I'm here with my son and my father to check out the new games.

Michelle: So who's the gamer in the family? Your son?

Man: Well, *actually* all three of us play . . .

Michelle: Really? So, what kind of games do *you* play?

Man: Me? Well, I like to play a role-playing game, online.

Michelle: A role-playing game . . . What do you like about it?

Man: Well, I like that you can play in a fantasy world. You can create your own character and make it look any way you want. Actually, my character is a woman.

Michelle: A woman? Really?

Man: Yeah, I heard that most men—like 70% of men in the game I play—make female characters for themselves.

Michelle: Well . . . what do you know . . .

Man: And your character does anything you want it to do—you can eat, sleep, dance . . . and walk around and talk to other characters.

Michelle: I see . . . so, it's kind of like living a fantasy life, huh?

Man: Yeah, kind of . . . and you work together with other players to fight battles and become stronger.

Michelle: So, you meet other players?

Man: Oh yeah, you play online, so millions of people can play, from all over. I even meet people from different countries, like Korea and Germany.

Michelle: Interesting. So, how about your son here? What kind of games do you like?

Boy: Well, I like action-adventure games. I think the most fun one is this game I play called *Legend of Zelda*.

Michelle: So what makes it fun?

Boy: First of all, it's exciting. You never know what's going to happen next. You play a character—he's a boy—and you explore different places, like forests and caves.

Michelle: So you just explore?

Boy: Oh no—there's a lot more to it than that. To win the game, you have to save the princess, but first you have to solve puzzles and stuff. You also find weapons and use them to fight battles against monsters along the way. So, it's challenging. That makes it fun, too.

Michelle: Sounds like that game is a little violent for a kid your age, don't you think?

Boy: Well . . . I don't know about that . . .

Michelle: OK, so how about you? You must be the grandfather, right? What kind of games do you play?

Grandfather: I really like puzzle games. My favorite game is called *Tetris*.

Michelle: So how does that work?

Grandfather: You have to put shapes together and the game gets faster and faster as you go, so you have to move quickly. I like it because it's good for your coordination.

Michelle: And do you play any other games?

Grandfather: Sure. I also play a word game—where you put letters together to make words. A lot of my friends like to play puzzle games, too. I like them because they make you think. You know, some doctors even say playing games can help you keep your mind young and active.

Michelle: So do you think it's working? Is it keeping your mind young?

Grandfather: Well . . . I hope so! The only problem is it sure is easy to get addicted to these games—sometimes I just can't stop playing!

Michelle: Well, what do you know? I guess gaming really is for everybody. Back to you, Brad.

LISTEN FOR DETAILS

(Repeat Listen for Main Ideas)

MAKE INFERENCES

Excerpt One

Man: Oh, I think it's great. I'm here with my son and my father to check out the new games.

Michelle: So who's the gamer in the family? Your son?

Man: Well, actually all three of us play . . .

Reporter: Really?

Excerpt Two

Man: Well, I like that you can play in a fantasy world. You can create your own character and make it look any way you want. Actually, my character is a woman.

Michelle: A woman? Really?

Man: Yeah, I heard that most men—like 70% of men in the game I play—make female characters for themselves.

Michelle: Well . . . what do you know . . .

Excerpt Three

Boy: To win the game you have to save the princess, but first you have to solve puzzles and stuff. You also find weapons and use them to fight battles against monsters along the way. So, it's challenging. That makes it fun, too.

Michelle: Sounds like that game is a little violent for a kid your age, don't you think?

Boy: Well . . . I don't know about that . . .

2B. LISTENING TWO: *Do You Like Video Games, Too?*

Maria: Hi Jennifer.

Jennifer: Oh, hi Maria.

Kelly: Hi.

Maria: So what are you doing today?

Jennifer: Well, you know, the guys are out at that gaming expo, so Kelly and I are going to go shopping.

Maria: There's a gaming expo in town? Oh, I'm glad my son didn't ask to go . . . I can't stand those games he's always playing.

Jennifer: Well, you know not *all* games are bad . . .

Maria: I guess not. But he spends so much time playing. I'm always trying to get him to do other things, but he just wants to play his video games all the time. And some of them are so violent! Oh well, I guess it's just a boy thing.

Jennifer: Well . . . I don't know about that . . . Kelly and I both like to play games too, you know.

Maria: Oh yeah? What games do *you* play?

Jennifer: Well, I like to play a simulation game called the Sims.

Maria: The Sims?

Jennifer: Yeah, it's this game where you can design your own house. You can make it any way you want—mine has beautiful gardens and two swimming pools!

Maria: Really?

Jennifer: Yeah, and you can also create your own family and take care of them and see what happens to them. I like it because it's not about fighting, or winning battles, or even winning at all. You can just be creative. It's also challenging to take care of all the people you create and make them happy. That's what *I* like about it.

Maria: Huh . . . that does sound kind of fun. And Kelly, you play games, too?

Kelly: Yeah, I like music, so I mostly play music games, like karaoke. I think my favorite is my dancing game though.

Maria: A dancing game? How does that work?

Kelly: Well, you pick a song and then you follow the music and the dance steps with your feet. The better you can follow along, the more points you win. It's really fun, and the best thing is it's active. It's really good exercise! Not like most other video games. You should try it sometime.

Maria: Well . . . maybe I will!

3C. SPEAKING

PRONUNCIATION: *Joining Words Together*

Exercise 2

A: How often do you go out to eat?

B: Several times a week. How about you?

A: Almost always. It's easy and it's convenient.

B: I agree. But sometimes I like to cook.

A: You know how to cook? How about cooking dinner for me some evening?

B: Well, just invite yourself over! But yeah, that's OK. How about this weekend? Saturday?

A: Sounds great! You know, I'm addicted to chocolate.

B: I'm afraid I'm not a baker. How about chocolate ice cream?

UNIT 7: Good-Mood Foods

2A. LISTENING ONE: *Street Talk*

Larry: Mmm, it tastes delicious. What's in it?

Dan: Well, thanks. I hope it works. I'll try anything.

Larry: On the radio? No, thanks.

Dan: Oh, my girlfriend just left me, and now I'm all alone.

Barbara: Are you kidding?! I'm in a big hurry. I don't have time for this!

LISTEN FOR MAIN IDEAS

Host: Good afternoon and welcome to *Street Talk,* the radio show where we talk to people on the street. I'm your host, Marty Moore, the *Street Talk* guy. Today, I'm here on Market Street talking to people about food. Did you know that eating some foods can actually change your moods? That's right! Some doctors say that if you're in a bad mood, you can eat a certain food and the food will make you feel better. So let's talk to some people and see what *they* think about food and moods. Here's someone now. Hi. I'm Marty Moore, the *Street Talk* guy. What's your name?

Larry: Me? My name's Larry. Why?

Host: Nice to meet you, Larry. Would you like to be on the radio?

Larry: On the radio? No, thanks. I think I'm too nervous for that.

Host: Oh, don't be nervous. Here, have some of this soup. It will help you relax.

Larry: Soup? Mmm, it smells delicious. What's in it?

Host: It's made with chili peppers.

Larry: Wow! That's hot!

Host: Oh, don't worry. Soon you'll feel better. You see, chili peppers have something in them that makes your mouth feel very hot right after you eat them. But they will also help you to relax. The more chili peppers you eat, the more relaxed you will feel.

Larry: I sure hope you're right!

Host: OK, on to the next person. Hi, I'm Marty Moore. What's your name?

Dan: I'm Dan.

Host: Gosh Dan, you look *really* unhappy. What's wrong?

Dan: Oh, my girlfriend just left me, and now I'm all alone. I feel miserable!

Host: Gee, I'm sorry to hear that. Maybe I can help you feel better. Here. Eat some of these chocolate chip cookies. You see, chocolate has something in it that makes you feel more upbeat. Some people even say chocolate can make you feel like you're in love!

Dan: In love? Really?

Host: Yes, and cookies are also made with wheat flour. Wheat can help you to relax and feel more upbeat, too.

Dan: Well, thanks. I hope it works. I'll try anything.

Host: Good luck. OK, let's talk to someone else . . . hello. What's your name?

Barbara: My name? I'm Barbara. Who wants to know anyway?

Host: Well, I'm Marty Moore, the *Street Talk* guy. Would you like to be on the radio?

Barbara: Are you kidding?! I'm in a big hurry. I don't have time for this!

Host: Wow! You're in a bad mood. What's the matter?

Barbara: Sorry, but I'm really stressed! I'm late for work, and I'm still waiting for the bus! I hope it gets here soon. I have a lot of work to do, and my boss is going to be angry!

Host: Here, I've got just what you need. Eat this turkey sandwich, and drink this glass of orange juice.

Barbara: A turkey sandwich and orange juice? Are you crazy? I need a bus, not food!

Host: Hey, don't be so irritable. I'm just trying to help. You see, turkey can help you to feel more energetic so you can do all of your work and feel less stressed. And the vitamin C in your orange juice can also help you to feel more energetic. It can even help you to feel more upbeat so you won't be so irritable.

Barbara: Thanks anyway, but I don't have time for food. I have to get to work!

Host: Well, our time's up for today. This is Marty, the *Street Talk* guy, saying good-bye for now. And don't forget—eat the right foods, and stay in a good mood.

LISTEN FOR DETAILS

(Repeat Listen for Main Ideas)

MAKE INFERENCES

Excerpt One

Host: Oh, don't be nervous. Here, have some of this soup. It will help you relax.

Larry: Soup? Mmm, it smells delicious. What's in it?

Host: It's made with chili peppers.

Larry: Wow! That's hot!

Excerpt Two

Barbara: I'm late for work, and I'm still waiting for the bus! I hope it gets here soon. I have a lot of work to do, and my boss is going to be angry!

Host: Here, I've got just what you need. Eat this turkey sandwich, and drink this glass of orange juice.

Barbara: A turkey sandwich and orange juice? Are you crazy? I need a bus, not food!

2B. LISTENING TWO: *What's the Matter?*

Narrator: What's the matter, Kate?

Kate: Oh, boy. Tomorrow's the big day. I'm getting married! I'm excited, but I'm really nervous, too. I hope I'm not making a mistake! I hope nothing goes wrong at the wedding!

Narrator: What's the matter, Derek?

Derek: Oh, my gosh, I'm totally stressed out. I have so much to do! I have to stay late at my job tonight to finish my work. Then I have to go to my son's school. He's in a play. I hope I can get there on time!

Narrator: What's the matter with Jane?

Jane: Hello? . . . What? No, he doesn't live here. You have the wrong number!

Ooooh, I hate it when people call and wake me up when I'm sleeping! And it really irritates me when it's a wrong number! How can people be so rude! Now I'll never get back to sleep!

Narrator: What's the matter, Jeff?

Jeff: I can't believe I just failed *another* math test. How stupid of me! And I needed a good grade on this test to pass the class . . . I feel miserable. What am I going to do?

UNIT 8: An Ice Place to Stay

2A.   LISTENING ONE: *An Unusual Vacation*

Recorded Voice: Thank you for calling the Swedish travel telephone hotline. We have information about transportation, lodging, and tourist activities in Sweden. For information about transportation, press 1. For lodging, press 2, and for tourist activities, press 3.

You've pressed 2 for information about lodging in Sweden. To hear more about campsites, press 1. For small inns, press 2, for large hotels press 3, and for information about a special hotel in Sweden, press 4.

You've pressed 4 for a special hotel in Sweden. If you'd like to hear recorded information, press 1. If you'd like to talk with an agent, press 2.

You've pressed 2. Please hold . . .

LISTEN FOR MAIN IDEAS

Recorded Voice: Thank you for calling the Swedish travel telephone hotline. We have information about transportation, lodging, and tourist activities in Sweden. For information about transportation, press 1. For lodging, press 2, and for tourist activities, press 3.

You've pressed 2 for information about lodging in Sweden. To hear more about campsites, press 1. For small inns, press 2, for large hotels, press 3, and for information about a special hotel in Sweden, press 4.

You've pressed 4 for a special hotel in Sweden. If you'd like to hear recorded information, press 1. If you'd like to talk with an agent, press 2.

You've pressed 2. Please hold . . .

Woman: Hello. May I help you?

Man: Yes. Could you tell me more about the special hotel in Sweden?

Woman: Sure. That's the Ice Hotel. It's located in a small town in Swedish Lapland, inside the Arctic Circle. So, when would you like to go?

Man: Well, I'm looking for a winter vacation.

Woman: Perfect! In fact, the Ice Hotel is only open in the winter because it's made of ice and snow.

Man: Ice and snow?

Woman: That's right. It's built out of ice and snow every November when the weather's cold. Then in the spring, it melts—it turns into water when the weather gets warm.

Man: Sounds cold!

Woman: Well, you're right, it is cold. Outside, the temperature is sometimes 40 degrees below freezing. It's warmer inside the hotel though—about five degrees below freezing Celsius.

Man: Wait a minute. Did you say *five below freezing?* . . . What is that in Fahrenheit?

Woman: Well, that's about 23 degrees Fahrenheit.

Man: Is it that cold in the rooms?!

Woman: Yes, but . . .

Man: Oh! . . . So people really stay there?!

Woman: Sure. The Ice Hotel is really popular with travelers from all over the world. Every year, different artists create the rooms and furniture, and it's decorated with beautiful ice sculptures. Adventurous travelers like to stay there because it's beautiful and it's unusual. It's really an exciting experience!

Man: Oh my . . . I see. It does sound interesting . . . So what are the rooms like?

Woman: Well, the guest rooms all have tall beds that are made of ice and snow and covered with reindeer furs. To stay warm at night, you sleep in a very warm sleeping bag. And you'll need to wear your hat to keep your ears warm! There are a few things the rooms don't have though—for one thing, they don't have bathrooms. You have to go to another building to use the bathroom. There also aren't any closets for your clothes. Your clothes would freeze!

Man: Oh . . . So how much does it cost to stay there?

Woman: The cheapest room is about 2500 Swedish Krona, which is about $350 a night.

Man: 350? For the *cheapest* room? You're kidding me!

Woman: Well . . . I know it's a little expensive, but it's definitely worth it.

Man: OK. . . If you say so . . . So what can you do there?

Woman: Well, there are some other rooms to visit at the hotel. If you like art, you can look at some paintings in the hotel's art gallery. There's a theater there where you can see a play. There's also a small church, and some guests even get married there.

Man: Well, I'm not planning to get married. Is there anything else I can do there?

Woman: Oh yeah, there are a lot of activities you can do near the Ice Hotel. There's a small museum you can visit to learn about the local history and culture. If you like winter activities, you can go cross-country skiing or snowshoeing. The exercise will warm you up! You can also go dogsledding or snowmobiling. And you can explore the wilderness and enjoy the beautiful arctic scenery. You might even see the Northern Lights while you're there.

Man: The Northern Lights?! Oh, I would love to see that!

Woman: Great! So would you like to make a reservation?

Man: Well . . . I'll think about it . . .

Woman: OK. I hope you'll decide to visit the Ice Hotel. I'm sure you'll have a great time!

Man: Thanks . . . bye!

LISTEN FOR DETAILS

(Repeat Listen for Main Ideas.)

MAKE INFERENCES

Excerpt One

Woman: Well, you're right, it is cold. Outside, the temperature is sometimes 40 degrees below freezing. It's warmer inside the hotel though—about five degrees below freezing Celsius.

Man: Wait a minute. Did you say *five below freezing?* . . . What is that in Fahrenheit?

Woman: Well, that's about 23 degrees Fahrenheit.

Man: Is it that cold in the rooms?!

Excerpt Two

Man: Oh! . . . So people really stay there?!

Woman: Sure. The Ice Hotel is really popular with travelers from all over the world. Every year, different artists create the rooms and furniture, and it's decorated with beautiful ice sculptures. Adventurous travelers like to stay there because it's beautiful and it's unusual. It's really an exciting experience!

Man: Oh my . . . I see. It does sound interesting . . .

Excerpt Three

Man: So how much does it cost to stay there?

Woman: The cheapest room is about 2500 Swedish Krona, which is about $350 a night.

Man: 350? For the *cheapest* room? You're kidding me!

Woman: Well . . . I know it's a little expensive, but it's definitely worth it.

2B. LISTENING TWO: *Vacations around the World*

Vacation 1

This travel package takes you to sunny and warm southern California. Visit the world famous Disneyland amusement park and have the time of your life! When you aren't having fun at Disneyland, you can go sightseeing and take a tour of Hollywood. Maybe you'll even see some movie stars! You can also go shopping in Los Angeles or visit the art museums. Price includes four nights lodging at the Disneyland Hotel and bus tours of all the sights. Travel anytime!

Vacation 2

This tour is for the adventurous traveler who loves the outdoors. Go hiking through the Himalayan Mountains of Nepal, and go swimming in the rivers. Enjoy the beautiful views. On this trip, you'll sleep outdoors in a campsite and meet other travelers from all over the world. You must be healthy for this vacation because you'll walk ten miles a day and carry your own sleeping bag and food. This price includes airfare, food, a tent and a sleeping bag, and a travel guide for your two-week adventure. This tour is offered in the spring or fall, when the days are warm and sunny and the nights are cool.

Vacation 3

On this vacation, you will enjoy the warm weather and meet the friendly people of Bali, Indonesia. While in Bali, you can relax on the beach. You can also learn about Balinese history, language, and culture. You can study art or dance with a local artist or you can learn how to cook Balinese food. On this trip, you will stay with a family in their home. One low price includes food and lodging. Airfare is extra. Travel in August or December.

3C. SPEAKING

PRONUNCIATION

Exercise 3

1. You can't go ice fishing.
2. You can't go shopping.
3. You can visit an old church.
4. You can't go in the summer.
5. You can go to a museum.
6. You can go cross-country skiing.

UNIT 9: Staying Healthy

2A.   LISTENING ONE: *Thin-Fast*

Man: So don't wait another minute. You should try Thin-Fast Diet Tea today. To order your Thin-Fast, call 1-800-555-THIN. That's 1-800-555-8446. Call today and get eight weeks of Thin-Fast for only $39.99. Yes, that's only $39.99 for the best weight-loss product money can buy. Call now and become happy, healthy, and thin!

LISTEN FOR MAIN IDEAS

Man: Are you overweight? Do you feel fat and unhealthy? Then you should try our amazing weight-loss remedy, Thin-Fast Diet Tea. Thin-Fast Diet Tea is a drink that will help you to lose weight fast. Here's one of our happy customers to tell you about it herself. Mary Ann, what do you think about Thin-Fast Diet Tea?

Mary Ann: Oh, it's terrific! It changed my life.

Man: Really? How did it change your life?

Mary Ann: Well, three months ago I was overweight and unhealthy. I ate fattening food and I never exercised. I looked terrible and I felt terrible. Before that, I had tried many different diets and weight-loss remedies, but nothing worked. I just couldn't lose weight. I was so unhappy! Then one day I decided to try Thin-Fast Diet Tea. It really worked! With Thin-Fast, I lost 65 pounds in only three months. Now I'm thin and happy. I feel healthy and energetic, and everyone says I look great!

Man: I agree! You look terrific, Mary Ann. So tell us, how do you use Thin-Fast?

Mary Ann: Oh, it's very easy to use. You just drink one cup of Thin-Fast twice a day, once in the morning and once in the evening. That's all! And the best part is, you don't have to exercise, and you don't have to go on a diet.

Man: Really? That sounds too good to be true. So, how does Thin-Fast work?

Mary Ann: Well, Thin-Fast helps you to lose weight in two different ways. First, it stops you from feeling hungry. After drinking a cup of Thin-Fast, you don't feel hungry, so you will eat less food and lose weight.

Man: Well, that's great. But with Thin-Fast do you have to stop eating fattening foods?

Mary Ann: Not at all! With Thin-Fast, you can eat all the fattening foods that you love, and you'll never gain weight. You see, the second way that Thin-Fast works is that it prevents your body from taking in the calories from foods that make you gain weight. With Thin-Fast, I ate chocolate and ice cream every day, I never exercised, and I still lost weight.

Man: That's just amazing, Mary Ann. But is Thin-Fast a healthy way to lose weight?

Mary Ann: Oh, yes. It's very safe and healthy. It doesn't have any side effects at all. In fact, in China people have safely used the natural ingredients in Thin-Fast to lose weight for 2,000 years.

Man: 2,000 years?

Mary Ann: That's right. And today, people still use it to lose weight.

Man: So, what's it made of? What are the ingredients of Thin-Fast?

Mary Ann: It's made from 100 percent natural herbs. There's nothing artificial in Thin-Fast.

Man: That's great, but I know that losing weight can make you feel tired. How do you feel when you drink Thin-Fast? Do you feel tired?

Mary Ann: Oh, no. The natural herbs in Thin-Fast will help you to feel more energetic, so you'll never feel tired or hungry.

Man: Wow! And how does Thin-Fast taste? Most diet drinks taste terrible.

Mary Ann: Oh, not Thin-Fast. It tastes great! It comes in two delicious flavors, orange and lemon. So losing weight is as easy as drinking a delicious cup of tea.

Man: That's wonderful, Mary Ann! Now I'm sure you'll agree that Thin-Fast is *the* fast and easy way to lose weight.

Mary Ann: That's right!

Man: So don't wait another minute. You should try Thin-Fast Diet Tea today. To order your Thin-Fast, call 1-800-555-THIN. That's 1-800-555-8446. Call today and get eight weeks of Thin-Fast for only $39.99. Yes, that's only $39.99 for the best weight-loss product money can buy. Call now and become happy, healthy, and thin!

LISTEN FOR DETAILS

(Repeat Listen for Main Ideas.)

MAKE INFERENCES

Excerpt One

Man: Really? How did it change your life?

Mary Ann: Well, three months ago I was overweight and unhealthy. I ate fattening food and I never exercised. I looked terrible and I felt terrible. Before that, I had tried many different diets and weight-loss remedies, but nothing worked. I just couldn't lose weight. I was so unhappy! Then one day I decided to try Thin-Fast Diet Tea. It really worked! With Thin-Fast, I lost 65 pounds in only three months. Now I'm thin and happy. I feel healthy and energetic, and everyone says I look great!

Excerpt Two

Man: I agree! You look terrific, Mary Ann. So tell us, how do you use Thin-Fast?

Mary Ann: Oh, it's very easy to use. You just drink one cup of Thin-Fast twice a day, once in the morning and once in the evening. That's all! And the best part is, you don't have to exercise, and you don't have to go on a diet.

Excerpt Three

Man: That's just amazing, Mary Ann. But is Thin-Fast a healthy way to lose weight?

Mary Ann: Oh, yes. It's very safe and healthy. It doesn't have any side effects at all. In fact, in China people have safely used the natural ingredients in Thin-Fast to lose weight for 2,000 years.

Man: 2,000 years?

Mary Ann: That's right. And today, people still use it to lose weight.

2B.   LISTENING TWO: *Being Healthy Is Good for You!*

Doctor: Hi. Well, I have your test results and, unfortunately, your blood pressure is a bit too high.

Patient: Oh . . . well . . . what does that mean?

Doctor: It means that you have a higher risk of heart problems.

Patient: Uh oh . . .

Doctor: But don't worry. I can give you a medication for this. But you should also try to lose some weight.

Patient: Well, you know, I've tried to lose weight in the past, but nothing worked.

Doctor: Hm . . . You know, there are a lot of reasons people can be overweight. Genetics can be one reason; something in your body that makes you more likely to become overweight.

Patient: Hm . . . so it's not the food that makes me gain weight?

Doctor: Well, it's *possibly* genetic. But having a healthy lifestyle is important, too.

Patient: OK . . .

Doctor: Basically, the way to lose weight and have a healthy lifestyle is to develop good habits. Good habits include eating less, having a healthy diet, and being more physically active. I can help you develop a plan for exercise and a healthy diet.

Patient: Well, is it *really* that important? I mean . . . well, wait a second, 'cause I really don't have time to exercise . . . and I don't want to give up the foods that I love.

Doctor: I understand but it's not just about losing weight. Being physically active keeps your heart healthy. Alright? It is also good for your bones and muscles. Also, you'll feel better and you'll sleep better. And you don't need to give up every food you love, only those that are fattening and high in calories. So I can give you a diet plan that has a lot of delicious meals and that are good for you and easy to make. You won't even miss the foods that are unhealthy for you.

Patient: OK, well, that sounds good. But I have to tell you, I hate going to the gym, and I'm too busy to exercise every day.

Doctor: Well, you don't have to go to the gym for two hours every day to get the exercise you need. The way to think about it is, be active.

Patient: OK . . .

Doctor: Many everyday activities are great ways to exercise—cleaning your house, working in your garden . . .

Patient: Hm. You mean cleaning my house is good for me?

Doctor: Absolutely! You can also try a few other ways to be active—take stairs instead of elevators or escalators, or next time you need to go to the store down the street, walk or ride your bicycle.

Patient: OK . . .

Doctor: Remember, only half an hour a day of exercise is enough to keep you healthy.

Patient: Wow, well that's definitely something I can do!

Doctor: Yes.

Patient: So let me ask you about this weight loss drink I read about. All you have to do is drink it. No need to diet or exercise and you lose all the weight you want. I mean, it sounds so easy. What do you think?

Doctor: Well, as a doctor I'll tell you that to be healthy and stay healthy, you need to eat right and exercise. OK? Eating anything you want *and* losing weight, it probably isn't true. It's hard work to stay healthy, but worth it . . . don't you think?

3C. SPEAKING

PRONUNCIATION: *Reductions*

Exercise 2

1. Rosa, you look so tired. What's the matter?
2. Did you know that Jim just lost his job? He's really upset.
3. My doctor said I really ought to lose weight, but I don't think I eat too much.

4. We need some time off. Life shouldn't be all work. We ought to have some fun.
5. My roommate has to study tonight, so you can't come over.
6. My computer's really slow. It's old, too. I think I have to get a new one.

a. You have to come to the gym with me. You'll lose weight just by exercising.
b. That's OK. I have to study, too. Let's get together this weekend.
c. I have to work late every night. I never get any sleep.
d. You ought to get a laptop. They're not expensive and they're very convenient.
e. You know I can't ask for a vacation now. I just started this job two weeks ago. I have to work longer.
f. He has to come to my office. My boss is looking for someone with his experience.

3C. SPEAKING

PRODUCTION

Man 1: Hey Jack. You got a sec?

Man 2: Yeah, sure. Come on in.

Man 1: Yeah, I was wondering if you . . . Jack! Your hair is on fire!

Man 2: Yeah, yeah, I know. I just need to finish this sales report and I'll probably, oh I don't know, maybe lie down for a bit. But I'm sure it'll go away.

Man 1: But the flames are getting bigger! Shouldn't I . . . Your hair! There's so much fire!

Man 2: No, no, I'll be fine. What can I help you with? Oh dear. Well, at least we know the sprinkler system works.

Announcer: You wouldn't ignore this, so why ignore the signs of a stroke? If you, or someone you know, suddenly experiences numbness of the face, arm, or leg, or sudden trouble speaking, seeing, or walking, don't wait to get help. Call 911 right away. Because time lost is brain lost. To find out more, visit www.strokeassociation.org or call 1-888-4 STROKE. This message brought to you by the American Stroke Association and the Ad Council.

UNIT 10: Endangered Languages

2A. LISTENING ONE: *Language Loss*

Professor: Good morning, everybody. Today, I'd like to talk about endangered and dead languages. So . . . who did the reading for today?
Hm . . . I see . . . *some* of you did. . . . Then, who can tell me what a dead language is?

LISTEN FOR MAIN IDEAS

Professor: Good morning, everybody. Today, I'd like to talk about endangered and dead languages. So . . . who did the reading for today?
Hm . . . I see . . . *some* of you did. . . . Then, who can tell me what a dead language is?

Student 1: Um . . . Is it a language that nobody speaks anymore, you know, like Latin?

Professor: Yeah, that's right. Now, how about an endangered language? Jessica, what do you think?

Student 2: An endangered language? Well, uh . . . maybe it's a language that *might* die?

Professor: Right. An endangered language is a language that may die, or become extinct soon. There are over 6,000 languages in the world, and some linguists think that 90 percent could be extinct by the year 2100. (*pause* . . .) Yes, that's a lot! So, many linguists want to preserve these dying languages.

Student 2: So, why do they want to do that? There are so many languages! Isn't it easier when people speak the same language anyway?

Professor: Well, that's a good point. Having fewer languages is more convenient for communication, but there are good reasons to save endangered languages. When a language dies, part of the culture can die, too. Now this doesn't always happen. For instance, the Manx people on the Isle of Man in the Irish Sea lost their native language, but they've kept their culture and traditions as Manx. But think about what is expressed through language: stories, ceremonies, poetry, humor, a whole way of thinking and feeling. When a language dies, all of this may be lost. So, culture is lost. Also, history and knowledge are passed down through language, so when the language disappears, important history and knowledge may be lost, too. So that's why people care about language loss. All right . . . moving on . . . Now, how do you think languages become endangered and extinct?

Student 3: Well, I guess nobody speaks them or studies them.

Professor: Yes. And this happens for several reasons. Sometimes the government makes it illegal to teach the language in school. For example, before 1987, it was illegal to teach the Hawaiian language in Hawaii's public schools. It was difficult for children to learn Hawaiian. As a result, that language became endangered. Starting in 1987, new programs began to teach the Hawaiian language. Today, there are more than 2,000 students enrolled in these programs.

In another situation, if one community has more power than another community, the less powerful community often feels it must learn the language of the more powerful group. Two things can happen in this situation. In one case, the more powerful language replaces the other language. One example is the case of Native American languages spoken in what is now the United States. Once, there were hundreds of Native American languages. Now, more and more people speak English, and not the native languages. Many of these languages have become extinct.

So, sometimes a community totally replaces their native language with another language. Or, the less powerful community can keep their native language and learn the other language, too. An example of this is in Greenland where students learn Kalaallisut and Danish. They are bilingual; they learn both languages, so they won't lose their native language. Also, Kalaallisut was made an official language in Greenland, along with Danish. This can also help save endangered languages for future generations.

Student 3: So . . . Are people doing anything else to save the dying languages?

Professor: Yes, linguists help create community programs where people can study the language and learn about the culture. Also, they try to preserve as many endangered languages as they can. They make videotapes, audiotapes, and written records of language with translations. They also study the vocabulary and rules of the language, and write dictionaries and grammar books.

OK, that's a lot of information for one lecture! We talked about endangered and dying languages and why it's important to save languages, how languages die, and how people can save endangered languages. Great! So for next time, please read chapter ten.

LISTEN FOR DETAILS

(Repeat Listen for Main Ideas)

MAKE INFERENCES

Excerpt One

Professor: Good morning everybody. Today, I'd like to talk about endangered and dead languages. So . . . who did the reading for today? Hm . . . I see *some* of you did . . .

Excerpt Two

Professor: Now, how about an endangered language? Jessica, what do you think?

Jessica: An endangered language? . . .Well, uh . . . maybe it's a language that *might* die?

Excerpt Three

Professor: But think about what is expressed through language: stories, ceremonies, poetry, humor, a whole way of thinking and feeling. When a language dies, all of this may be lost. So, culture is lost.

Also, history and knowledge are passed down through language, so when the language disappears, important history and knowledge may be lost, too. So that's why people care about language loss.

All right . . . moving on . . . Now, how do you think languages become endangered and extinct?

2B.   LISTENING TWO: *My Life, My Language*

Woman: I am Maori, living in New Zealand. In school, I learned and spoke English; it was the official language. Everything was taught in English in school. That was the government policy. I only heard Maori when I was with my grandparents. I could understand a little Maori, but could not speak it. I could not have a conversation with my grandparents because they did not speak English.

When I was in school, I knew that I was not learning the Maori culture, and I felt separated from my grandparents because of that. I felt empty inside and different from my family.

Maori is an endangered language and if children stop learning it, it will die. I do not want to see Maori disappear. So now that I am an adult and have children of my own, I decided I wanted my children to learn their native language. I found a pre-school that teaches children Maori before they enter school where they will learn English. The schools are called "language nests." In 1981, a group of Maori leaders saw that Maori was endangered and dying. They decided to do something. They did not want to wait for the government to do anything, so they got together and came up with the idea of pre-schools where children could learn Maori. Now, there are over 700 language nests and more than 13,000 children who are bilingual in Maori and English. Language nests are a big part of Maori education. Also in 1987, the government recognized Maori as the official language of New Zealand, with English, too.

The children learn the basic values of the Maori culture. We have a strong belief in love, compassion, caring, hospitality, family responsibilities, and respect for elders. Children also learn our Maori stories. And through the language nests, children learn these values, as well as the language.

I also wanted to learn more about my language and culture. Now, there are classes for adults like me. The teachers are all older Maoris, usually grandparents. We meet in neighborhood centers. There are also week-long classes where adults can go and study. In these courses, no English is spoken all week! Everything is Maori. The programs are good because now there are many more adults who speak Maori. It helps our children who are also learning Maori.

THE PHONETIC ALPHABET

Consonant Symbols

/b/	**b**e		/t/	**t**o
/d/	**d**o		/v/	**v**an
/f/	**f**ather		/w/	**w**ill
/g/	**g**et		/y/	**y**es
/h/	**h**e		/z/	**z**oo, bu**s**y
/k/	**k**eep, **c**an		/θ/	**th**anks
/l/	**l**et		/ð/	**th**en
/m/	**m**ay		/ʃ/	**sh**e
/n/	**n**o		/ʒ/	vi**s**ion, A**s**ia
/p/	**p**en		/tʃ/	**ch**ild
/r/	**r**ain		/dʒ/	**j**oin
/s/	**s**o, **c**ircle		/ŋ/	lo**ng**

Vowel Symbols

/ɑ/	**fa**r, h**o**t		/iy/	**we**, m**ea**n, f**ee**t
/ɛ/	m**e**t, s**ai**d		/ey/	d**ay**, l**a**te, r**ai**n
/ɔ/	t**a**ll, b**ou**ght		/ow/	g**o**, l**ow**, c**oa**t
/ə/	s**o**n, **u**nder		/uw/	t**oo**, bl**ue**
/æ/	c**a**t		/ay/	t**i**me, b**uy**
/ɪ/	sh**i**p		/aw/	h**ou**se, n**ow**
/ʊ/	g**oo**d, c**oul**d, p**u**t		/oy/	b**oy**, c**oi**n

CREDITS